WHAT PEOPLE ARE SAYING ABOUT CHRIS PALMER AND *LETTERS FROM JESUS*...

Learning Greek language insight into God's Word was absolutely foundational in building my faith and ministry so many years ago as a student—insights which serve me to this day. That's why I am so pleased to recommend *Letters from Jesus*. Chris Palmer has an outstanding gift in bringing alive God's Word, providing an invaluable upgrade in understanding and empowerment, much needed for this generation. Who knew Greek insight could be this enriching and enjoyable! Thank you, Chris. Your passion and precision have served up an excellent study!

—*Sy Rogers*
International communicator and pastoral care specialist
Director, Sy Rogers Communications

Letters from Jesus makes accessible, to every believer, a book of the New Testament often avoided—the book of Revelation. Chris Palmer offers 52 studies from the Greek text that will be a delight for every reader. In these studies, Chris leads his readers through a portion of text from the letters to the churches of Revelation while mining spiritual insights from the Greek text that are colorfully illustrated with warm personal stories and encouraging words from a pastor's heart. These studies are sure to be a blessing to many. My only hope is that another book is forthcoming!

—*Philip L. Mayo, Ph.D.*
Professor, New Testament and Greek
Director, School of Biblical and Theological Studies
North Central University, Minneapolis, MN

This practical and helpful study uncovers keen truths and insights only found through a close reading of the Greek text. Chris Palmer's readings bring to the fore the social implications of these all-too-often overlooked portions of the New Testament. His work offers a methodologically rich framework for understanding the seven letters of Jesus in Revelation 2–3. His avoidance of technical jargon fills a gap for busy pastors and laypersons who desire to keep their devotional literature close to the text rather than surface-level ideas read into it.

—*J. Brian Tucker, Ph.D.*
Moody Theological Seminary

Reading Chris Palmer's *Letters from Jesus* is like attending a series of encouraging, deep-dive Bible studies led by an expert in the original language of the New Testament. Chris has a rare, welcoming approach to help you to explore and reflect upon the original meaning of the text. You don't have to know Greek to start reading and enjoying this book, but you will know some by the time you're done.

—*Dr. John Schwandt*
Institute of Biblical Greek
Creator, National Biblical Greek Exam
General Editor, *ESV English-Greek Reverse Interlinear New Testament*

Not so long ago, the study of biblical languages was considered essential for ministerial preparation. For understandable reasons—namely, the time and effort it takes to gain mastery over the structures of a language—such a goal has been deemed even by theological educators to be not worth the effort, often settling for namesake attempts in that direction. It is true that we can understand much, even beyond the essentials, by studying the Bible in translation, just as one can enjoy and understand Shakespeare in translation. But just as no one will deny that reading Shakespeare in translation is not the same as appreciating fully what the Bard wrote, so also, the case for reading the biblical text in the original needs no championing. Chris Palmer demonstrates that well in *Letters from Jesus* by presenting lexical and grammatical insights from his journey through the Greek text of the letters to the seven churches in Revelation 2 and 3, and he does so in an interesting, accessible, and inviting manner.

—*Professor Raju Kunjummen, Th.M.*
Chair, Bible and Theology Department
Emmaus Bible College, Dubuque, IA
Author, *New Testament Greek: A Whole Language Approach*

CHRIS PALMER

LETTERS
Επιστολές από τον Ιησού
FROM JESUS

STUDIES FROM THE
SEVEN CHURCHES OF REVELATION

WHITAKER
HOUSE

LETTERS FROM JESUS
Studies from the Seven Churches of Revelation

Light of Today Ministries
www.lightoftoday.com
www.instagram.com/chrispalmer

ISBN: 978-1-64123-310-1
eBook ISBN: 978-1-64123-311-8
Printed in the United States of America
© 2019 by Chris Palmer

Whitaker House
1030 Hunt Valley Circle
New Kensington, PA 15068
www.whitakerhouse.com

Library of Congress Cataloging-in-Publication Data (Pending)

1 2 3 4 5 6 7 8 9 10 11 ⊔⊔ 26 25 24 23 22 21 20 19

To Prof. Raju Kunjummen and Dr. J. Brian Tucker

Εὐχαριστῶ τῷ θεῷ μου ἐπὶ πάσῃ τῇ μνείᾳ ὑμῶν.

ACKNOWLEDGMENTS

Like many of life's meaningful undertakings, *Greek for the Week* didn't happen overnight. It's a product that has been in the making for almost fifteen years—since I walked into my first Greek class at North Central University in September 2005. It was a struggle. But my professor, Dr. Phil Mayo, saw me through. For that, I shall give Dr. Mayo and NCU the first thank you.

After earning my bachelor's degree, my interest in Greek lay dormant for nearly seven years until it was awakened by Dr. John Schwandt and his Institute for Biblical Greek. So, for that he gets the second thanks.

Immediately after my time learning under Dr. Schwandt, I decided to deepen my studies in Greek and earn a master's at Moody Theological Seminary. Here, I met Prof. Raju Kunjummen and Dr. J. Brian Tucker. I'm not sure these professors will ever know the impact their teaching has had upon my thinking and, ultimately, my faith. Their classes were the highlight of my week for a number of years. I often think back to their classes and miss them...a lot. These two professors, along with Moody Theological Seminary, get the third thank you.

Around the end of my time at Moody, *Greek for the Week* became an idea: I could teach God's Word from the Greek in an easy and applicable way to an everyday, online audience! The only problem was, I didn't have much of an online audience. The Lord brought Sergio Alvarado along. Serg helped me develop my online platform so that *Greek for the Week* could reach the eyes and hearts of thousands of people every week. Thanks, bro!

Next, it's fitting to thank Stephanie Camargo. Steph, you helped me solve many problems as *Greek for the Week* began taking shape. You enabled me to craft a vision for this concept and set it into motion. *Grazie, Mille!*

As *Greek for the Week* became a common post in people's feeds, I'd often get asked who was behind the camera filming me. "The Greek Squad," of course: Brittany Cosby and Beshar Shukri. These two faithful comrades of mine worked with me patiently after church on Sundays and helped do take, after take, after take...after take. (I think our longest film session took 131!) And they never complained, not once. Thank you!

Greek for the Week eventually turned into this book because of the help of Luana Minutella. Thank you for all your patience and hard work. I don't think we will ever settle on what the term "drip pan" means.

After it became a book, my editor, Mary Achor, polished it up and gave it the "Mary Magic," as I often call it. Thank you, Mary. I've learned so much from you over the years.

Here's a good place to thank Whitaker House and their phenomenal team. You all are awesome and it's been so great working with you. Thank you for believing in *Greek for the Week*.

My church, Light of Today, deserves an enormous thanks. Having a loving and devoted congregation certainly made *Greek for the Week* a success. Thank you for lifting it up in all of our times of prayer. Within you, I see a church that the Lord Jesus is proud of.

Finally, the most important thank you goes to my family. What can I even begin to say, other than you have been my biggest fans, even during the times I wasn't a fan of myself. I love you dearly and this book couldn't have been accomplished without your love and support.

To the *Greek for the Week* family, a heartfelt thank you:

Ευχαριστώ!

CONTENTS

III. THE CHURCH AT SMYRNA—STUDIES ON ENDURANCE

IV. THE CHURCH AT PERGAMUM—STUDIES ON WORLDVIEW

V. THE CHURCH AT THYATIRA—STUDIES ON HOLINESS

VI. THE CHURCH AT SARDIS—STUDIES ON THE HOLY SPIRIT

VII. THE CHURCH AT PHILADELPHIA—STUDIES ON CHRISTIAN LIVING

VIII. THE CHURCH AT LAODICEA—STUDIES ON FAITHFULNESS

FOREWORD

Chris Palmer has been on a journey with Jesus for quite a while now. In fact, Jesus is his journey, because Jesus is the "*hodos*" (Greek for "way"). Whatever we know of Christ, ultimately, as Father John Behr clearly asserts, we "know him by interpretation," and by that, he means the faithful interpretation of the Sacred Text.

Regardless of our personal "experiences," we always run into the danger of veering off course if we fail to keep three things closely held together: the Spirit, the Scriptures, and the Son of God. The Father's three-fold cord (as Len Sweet refers to this) intends that we be formed by the inter-relationship of all three, and to separate any one from the other is to be in unsound, unorthodox territory. Even with a resurrected Jesus standing in the presence of fearful disciples in the upper room, He still had to "open their minds to understand the Scriptures" (Luke 24:45). They couldn't recognize Him in their experience until they recognized Him in the Sacred Text.

Before Rome ruled the world, Alexander the Great had conquered it, and the result was that the entire empire under Alexander became "Hellenized" and had to learn to speak Greek. Even with Rome conquering Greece and speaking Latin, the "lingua franca" for most of the expansive territories conquered by Alexander became Greek. In the Providence of God, the New Testament epistles were written in the "lingua franca," Koine Greek. It is one thing to have a *Strong's Concordance* in your personal library. It is far more rewarding to learn how to work with the actual Greek texts of Scripture.

Chris Palmer is inviting you to do just that, and do it in a way that is easy to grasp and inspiring to experience. Trust the process Chris takes your through in "Greek for the Week." He's done a masterful job of explaining how the common Greek language of the Ancient Near East works. He then places you in the history of the seven letters written to the seven churches of Asia Minor in the book of Revelation, and through his working with the Greek text, takes you on a contextual journey that is faithful to the text, faithful to the Spirit who inspired the text, and faithful to the Son who is both the focus of the book of Revelation and the Voice addressing the seven churches by the Spirit.

Chris shows you how these seven letters are as relevant and timely today as they were for the first century churches to whom they were written—and who indeed grasped their significance for their time. The same Spirit that inspired the Sacred Text is forming and shaping you to interact with the Text so that you can truly see Jesus! May your reading of this book lead to a fresh encounter with the Christ who stands in the midst of the seven lampstands!

—*Bishop Mark J. Chironna*
Church On The Living Edge
Mark Chironna Ministries, Longwood, FL

WHY GREEK?

When I was a young boy, I begged my parents for a microscope. Finally, they cracked and gave me one for Christmas. I wasted no time putting everything I could find onto slides for examination. Oh, the discoveries I made! Seeing something up close opened up a whole new world and gave me an understanding I never might have had otherwise. I developed a new appreciation for strands of hair, insects, and leaves. Beyond the casual eye, it was clear that they were held together by divine order. Their spectacular compositions gave me the notion that the minute world of cells wasn't randomly tossed together. It was purposeful, intentional, and meaningful. It was for my good and God's glory.

However, times changed. My love for science was surpassed by my love for God's Word. My microscope was replaced by a tool that could help me examine the Scripture down to the finest detail: Koine Greek. Like my microscope, Koine Greek has delivered splendid findings to me. I have discovered that God's Word is not an ignorant document, haphazardly thrown together, without rhyme or reason. It is the product of heavenly brilliance and its fabric is sewn together with the finest care and the most breathtaking details. We just have to look closely to see them. And Koine Greek is the closest we can get.

"Koine" means "common." It refers to the common language of the Mediterranean area from 300 B.C. to 300 A.D. The writing of the New Testament took place during this time, so it makes sense that all twenty-seven books were originally written in Koine. Also during this time, there were several dialects, two of which were Attic Greek and Koine Greek.

Attic Greek came first. It was a prestige dialect, used by the learned. Dramatists like Sophocles and Aeschylus and philosophers like Plato and Aristotle wrote in Attic Greek. As the Greek culture spread, the Greek language became more relaxed. Koine emerged as the language of everyday, less formal people: fishermen, merchants, farmers, and soldiers. God saw fit to use the language of the everyday people to communicate His truth about Jesus Christ. The Gospels aren't just for the elite—they're for *all* people, from the least to the greatest.

As time has plodded on, the New Testament has been translated from Koine into over 1,500 languages. These translations can certainly be trusted. Expert translation societies work with diligence and care to preserve the meaning of God's Word as they move it from one language to the next. If you never studied Greek, you'd be just fine with the translation you are using.

So why study Greek? There are a number or reasons:

1. IT'S LIKE READING THE BIBLE IN HIGH DEF

Unlike English, Koine Greek doesn't need word order or right branching sentences to communicate meaning. For instance, if you were to translate Jude 1:19 into English, word from word from the Greek, it would say this: *"These are the ones who cause divisions, wordly, the Spirit not they have."* As English speakers, this seems out of sorts. And it *is* out of sorts for the English language. You might be able to bear it for one sentence, but imagine reading a whole chapter, book, or the entire New Testament this way.

So when translators place it into English, they turn it around a bit: *"It is these who cause divisions, worldly people, devoid of the Spirit."* Now it makes sense. The only disadvantage is that we lose a nuance. Because Koine Greek doesn't need word order, writers sometimes took advantage of this and positioned words they wanted to emphasize up front. By placing *Spirit* in front of *not they have*, Jude is highlighting the fact that the apostates, who claimed to be of God, did not have *the Holy Spirit* as they were claiming to have. (Its position up front acts like bold font.) While Jude makes this clear in other places in his letter, we lose out on a little bit of the tone. It hasn't changed the meaning—and God's Word remains inspired, infallible, and inerrant—but it's not as sharp outside of the Greek. That's why I say reading in Greek is like watching a movie in high definition. We are seeing exactly the same picture, but in Greek, we get to see more detail.

> Ancient Greek dramatists invented theater. The Greek verb "theater" (*theaomoi*) means "to look at or to behold." Next time you are watching a drama at the cinema, remember it all began in Greek!

2. YOU'LL KNOW YOUR STUFF BETTER

Digging into the Greek forces us to wrestle with the grammar and syntax. This can be arduous and it takes time. But the more you wrestle with a passage, the more confidence you'll have in who you are, and in what you preach and teach, because you've dealt with it in depth.

For instance, let's take Luke 10:18. Jesus has sent seventy-two disciples out to proclaim the kingdom and heal the sick. When they return, they tell the Lord about the wonderful results they saw, that they even cast out devils. Jesus replies, *"I saw Satan fall like lightning from heaven."* This typically gets preached as though Jesus was referring to Satan's pre-Adamic fall.

Stay with me here for just a moment.

If we examine the verb for "I saw" (*etheōroun*), we will discover it is in the imperfect tense, which portrays an action *as it is happening*, like "I was seeing" or "I was watching." What Jesus could very well be saying is that, at the same time as the ones He sent out were proclaiming God's kingdom and ousting demons, He was watching Satan's kingdom collapse. The imperfect tense makes a pretty good case for this.

Getting to the bottom of passages like this will help to remove any ambiguity that might stifle your confidence in the text and will end any timidity you might have in thinking about or explaining a verse. You'll be a better minister of God's Word for it.

3. IT REMOVES PERSONAL BIASES

As I have studied Greek over the years, there've been times when I've had to say goodbye to some pet beliefs of mine. Pet beliefs are non-salvific beliefs— those minor things that belief (or disbelief) in don't change our standing in Christ or in His Body—that we hold to for various personal reasons. It could have been Grandpa's favorite thing to say, part of our old pastor's best sermon, or something formed on our own. Whatever the reason, it's just not supported in God's Word.

I'll give you an example from my own journey. When I was young in the Lord, I used to think that the ferocious locusts found in Revelation 9:7–10 were referring to war helicopters, like the Boeing AH-64 Apache. But there's really no room for it in the Greek. First, I had to ask myself why I couldn't just accept that the locusts are ferocious supernatural forces of evil as they are portrayed to be. (I could. It's just that I saw an end-time movie once and the locusts were helicopters...)

Next, Revelation 9:2–3 says the locusts come from the smoke that originates in the bottomless pit and go *"on the earth."* "On" is the Greek preposition *eis*. It means "into, onto." If they are coming "into" and "onto" the earth from the bottomless pit, this means that unless they have Boeing AH-64 Apache helicopters in hell, John is describing evil, spiritual beings. The Greek helped me iron this out, as it has other wrinkles I've had over the years. And it still does so today.

4. IT CHECKS OUR MOTIVES

In our fast-moving world—where everything is competing for our attention and everyone has something to say—people look to God's Word for all the wrong reasons. They may want a quick fix, a flashy lesson, or just something to support their own opinion. But if we want to truly benefit from God's Word, we have to spend time with it and let it infuse into our hearts. Studying God's Word in the original language forces us to approach it with reverence and awe, humbling ourselves to obey what it says, whether it's something we want to hear or not.

If you're at a place in your life where you desire to examine God's Word even more deeply than you have already, I'd encourage you to pursue the study of Koine Greek. It won't be easy, but in the end, you'll have a microscope of your own that you can slide Scripture under any time you want—and you'll be amazed by the discoveries you make.

INTRODUCTION

The letters from Jesus in the book of Revelation, which date back to 95 A.D., have helped us make a fascinating discovery about civilization: life hasn't changed much over the last two millennia. Don't let the landscape of human advancement and achievement fool you into thinking that we are any different than our ancestors. We are the same.

The Lord's letters show us that vices and virtues don't disappear with the march of time. The evils that brought humans low in times of antiquity are the same that rope us in today. And sacred honor still bestows on us touches of divine endorsement in the twenty-first century. That is to say, Jesus's urgent message to his seven churches in the Asian Peninsula wasn't just timely for Greco-Romans and Jews. It's well-timed for humanity everywhere, as long as we occupy a mortal body that prays for redemption from all human evils.

JESUS IS STILL SPEAKING TO US

There is a reason to lift your head amidst the sorrow: Jesus has spoken. The Commander of the Kingdom of God has issued a message that addresses the challenges of being human and being saved. The message is served straight up, full of hard-to-swallow realities for those who have drunk from the waters of redemption and eternal life. (See John 4:14.) But it's a good message and sweet to our eternal well-being. The people of God will overcome. We will overcome the vanity and the self-love that perils the soul. We will overcome the lusts that entice our sensuality. Highest yet, we will overcome the fear that causes us to cower in the presence of death, the mysterious foe that awaits at the end of this life. We *have* overcome and we *will* overcome.

It's a message with promise: we will shine on past death. The power at work in us, that conqueror of fallenness, is proof of the splendor that awaits. So, we are in flux: a good today, but looking for a finer tomorrow. This is being a Christian, a Christ-follower, or as they would have said in 95 A.D., those who follow "the Way."

> Early Christians referred to themselves as those of "the Way." (See Acts 9:2; 24:14.) This refers to the "way" of salvation. (See Acts 16:17.) The Greek word for "way" (*hodos*) means "path" or "road." Early Christians proclaimed Jesus Christ and his gospel as the exclusive road to peace with God and everlasting life.

A little on the seven churches: they lie along the eastern side of the Asia Minor peninsula. (Today, Asia Minor is called Turkey.) These churches are relatively close to one another. You could travel between Pergamum and Sardis, the two farthest from each other, within four hours. (Of course, in 95 A.D., this would seem much further.) Although these were not the only churches in Asia Minor, they were hubs overseeing other mother churches.

Now, seven is a number that often represents completion and perfection throughout the Bible, so seven is significant. These seven letters are a complete message for the entire church.[1] We serve ourselves well to observe the message in its completeness, which is why I have broken the message down verse by verse. I encourage you to consider it, even if it's not speaking directly to you in this season of life. At least, it can speak to you indirectly somehow, I'm sure.

You might find a lot of yourself in one of the churches or a little of yourself in all of the churches. Whatever the case, ask the Holy Spirit for His help to overcome as you go through this. You'll discover prayers, activities, and other Scriptures at the end of each study to assist you. They will help you to "overcome" and "conquer."

OVERCOMING TECHNICAL CHALLENGES

Working with Greek and English texts simultaneously presents some technical challenges that I've tried to alleviate. At the beginning of each chapter, you'll find the Scripture I'm working with in English and the corresponding Greek text below it. I highlight the English and Greek words that we examine so they match and correspond with one another.

Within the study itself, when I mention the Greek words, I use transliteration. This is how the Greek word or phrase sounds using the English alphabet. My goal is to help you understand how the Greek is pronounced, without the actual Greek slowing you down.

If you find that the technical aspects of the language are, in fact, slowing down your reading, it will help you to glance over these and concentrate on the insights we find in the Greek. I don't believe that anything in *Letters from Jesus* is that complicated. I've tried to simplify the studies as much as possible.

However, if you are one of those rare readers who's interested in the hum-drum technicalities of the language, I've created endnotes just for you. These will give you more insights about the mechanics of Greek that I mention, in case you'd like to investigate further. If you plan to make a sermon out of these studies or use them in some other capacity, examining the end-notes should give you some additional insights.

A LITTLE HISTORY HERE AND THERE

Finally, I chose not to pile up a bunch of historical information about each church right up front. I didn't think you'd digest it if I just dropped it there, one big hunk. Instead, I sprinkled it throughout each study. A little here, a little there. The churches aren't the prime focus: the message is. And I pray it speaks to you, right here in this fast-paced, technological world.

Maranatha.

Μαρὰν ἀθα.

Chris Palmer

SEVEN CHURCHES OF
REVELATION

1. EPHESUS
2. SMYRNA
3. PERGAMUM
4. THYATIRA
5. SARDIS
6. PHILADELPHIA
7. LAODICEA

ISLAND OF PATMOS IS WHERE JOHN
RECEIVED THE VISION

TURKEY
(ASIA MINOR)

AEGEAN SEA

PATMOS

Greece

20 MI
50 KM

A NOTE ON THE SEVEN CHURCHES OF ASIA

WHY *THESE* CHURCHES?

Those who read Revelation—also known as the Apocalypse of John—often wonder why Jesus chose to write to *these* seven churches. There *were* other churches in Asia Minor in the first century. What was unique about Ephesus, Smyrna, Pergamum, Thyatira, Sardis, Philadelphia, and Laodicea?

This has been an interesting point of discussion in scholarship. While the conversation is still open for robust discussion, there are some ideas that are widely accepted. The ones I've included fall in between the range of highly probable and matter of fact.

- These seven churches were parent churches, overseeing other, smaller churches. Looking at this from a modern perspective, these seven churches had "satellite churches" that followed their leadership and direction. A message to these seven was a message to those under their "covering."

+ The variety of issues and situations going on in these seven churches provide a microcosm of the church at large. Together, they portray the scope of what Christian communities experience. Almost any individual or church community can identify with at least one of these seven churches.

+ *Seven* is the number that represents completion and perfection. As a whole, these seven messages present a complete and perfect message from Christ to His church. Their unique situations form a comprehensive collection of case studies. Christ uses these to construct the perfect sermon, which He hands down to generations of His followers to come.

SEVEN CHURCHES, THREE THEMES

There are three main themes within Christ's messages to the seven churches:

1. Warning for those tempted to assimilate with the ungodly culture (Ephesus, Pergamum, Thyatira)

2. Encouragement for those facing debilitating persecution (Smyrna, Philadelphia)

3. Rebuke for those who have grown complacent and smug due to wealth and success (Sardis, Laodicea)

First introduced in the messages to the seven churches, these themes run the course of Revelation and are dealt with in every single vision throughout the duration of the book, in chapters four through twenty-two. Hence, Revelation can be heard in three different ways. If you were assimilating with ungodly culture, the visions might freeze your plans and turn you toward repentance. If you were enduring persecution, the visions would be received as a source of comfort and encourage you forward. If you had become overly concerned about wealth and lulled into complacency by success, the visions might awaken you, readjust your perspective, and cause you to get your priorities straight.

This is why, even today, Christians have mixed feelings about Revelation. I've met people who are scared by it and others who are encouraged by it. Then again, I've met those who aren't sure what to think about Revelation, other than they have to *do* something! Can you see the wisdom of the Holy Spirit behind this? The point is, the situation of the seven churches of Revelation provides the context for us to understand the rest of the book.

SIGNIFICANT GEOGRAPHY

"Asia Minor" is often confused with modern-day Asia. Unless otherwise informed, it's possible to think that these churches are somewhere near China! But that's not the case. "Asia Minor" refers to what is now modern-day Turkey and these seven churches were located around the western part of this area.

If we look at the map, we notice Patmos first. The apostle John had been exiled to this tiny island as a political prisoner. Kept in chains, he was forced to bust rocks in the stone quarries under the scorching sun. His clothing was tattered and his rations sparse. But it was during this time of travail that John recorded Revelation and had it sent to the seven churches to be read.

The order in which John address the churches isn't random. It follows an old postal route. A courier would more than likely deliver the letters following this path.

But there is an even more interesting observation to be noted. In Revelation 1:12–16, John describes the vision he has of Jesus. He sees the resurrected Lord in the center of seven golden lampstands, which represent the seven churches. If we look at the map and imagine Christ standing in the center of the churches, we'll observe that we move around Him and His splendor as we read each message. This represents several things:

+ Christ is the center of everything at all times. He is the center of the messages to the seven churches, the center of the book of Revelation, the center of His church, the center of all preaching and teaching (or should be), the center of our communities, families, and relationships—the list just goes on.

+ If we desire to experience the fullness of Christ, we must fully accept what He is saying to these churches. Eliminating the parts of Scripture that confront sin, challenge cultural and political idolatry, and warn of coming judgment will give us an incomplete picture of who Jesus is. If we want to know Him, we can't cherry-pick from the things He says. Doing this is dangerous and God's Word is warning us about that here.

• We experience the fullness of Christ as a community. Loner Christians and churches that seek to isolate themselves from the rest of the Christian community should find it sobering that Christ appears in the midst of the seven churches. Just about every cult and dangerous doctrine began when maverick, dissident individuals or groups cut themselves off from other Christians. This should be an eye-opener for those who claim to follow Jesus, yet bash the rest of the Christian community. The truth is, we all need a church home, we all need a pastor, and we all need the company of other Christians. Christ expects us to work out our hurts and differences with love and mercy. Walking away from the body of Christ is not acceptable. You won't find Jesus among the world—He's in the midst of His people.

> The USA has numerous cities that share names with the seven churches: Ephesus, Georgia; Smyrna (Georgia, South Carolina, and Tennessee); Thyatira, Mississippi; Sardis (Georgia, Mississippi, and Ohio); and Philadelphia (Pennsylvania, Illinois, Indiana, Mississippi, New York, and Tennessee). There is also a city named Patmos in Arkansas. However, there are no cities in the USA named after Pergamum or Laodicea.

WHERE ARE THE SEVEN CHURCHES TODAY?

Ephesus: now the site of some of the most marvelous archaeological ruins in the world, including the amphitheater of Acts 19. Near the modern-day city of Selçuk.

Smyrna: now the site of Izmir, the third largest city in Turkey, with more than four million people.

Pergamum: ruins of ancient Pergamum now overlook the modern-day city of Bergama. The ruins include the ancient altar to Zeus.

Thyatira: ruins of ancient Thyatira are now found in Akhisar, home to more than 100,000 people.

Sardis: ruins of ancient Sardis include an Artemis temple and bathhouse. They are located just a mile from the city of Sart.

Philadelphia: not much remains of the ancient city and church of Philadelphia. The site is now home to the city of Alaşehir.

Laodicea: ruins of ancient Laodicea are found near the city of Denizli. These ruins include streets, colonnades, and a well-preserved stadium.

PART I

THE VISION OF JESUS CHRIST—A STUDY ON THE WORD OF GOD

1

SOCIETY'S FADS DON'T CHANGE GOD'S WORD

John to the seven churches that are in Asia: Grace to you and peace from him who is and who was and who is to come...
                                                        (Revelation 1:4a)

Ἰωάννης ταῖς ἑπτὰ ἐκκλησίαις ταῖς ἐν τῇ Ἀσίᾳ· χάρις ὑμῖν καὶ εἰρήνη ἀπὸ ὁ ὢν καὶ ὁ ἦν καὶ ὁ ἐρχόμενος...
                                        (ΑΠΟΚΑΛΥΨΙΣ ΙΩΑΝΝΟΥ 1:4a)

Every day, apps update on my phone. I have mixed feelings about them. On one hand, it's satisfying to watch the app click its way into color as I anticipate new features that could smooth my life. On the other hand, I feel like these apps are too needy. *Coffee app, why do you demand to be updated just when I'm in line to pay? Don't do this now, Marco Polo, I was just getting* the hang of you. *More bugs, Viber? iTunes, is changing my terms of service going to be a monthly ritual?* And, of course, I can't open my laptop without a prompt that something needs to be changed *right now. More change in less time*: it's the technology revolution.

The speed at which information and ideas now travel has made an even greater revolution possible: the social revolution. Within twenty minutes of browsing Periscope for the first time, I had joined a group of Italian twenty-somethings hanging out under the Eiffel Tower, I was greeted by high school students in Kyrgyzstan when I joined their lecture, I watched an American clarinet teacher in South Korea teach jazz to his students, and I was welcomed by socialites in Saudi.

Closing the app felt like I was jumping out of my phone back into my bedroom. *Did that really happen?* I was distressed. *Where's this leading? What will society become? What have we already become?* The sands of society are being restyled by the waves of change.

Seven (*hepta*) is used to represent completion all over the Bible. Here are just a few examples: seven days in the creation account (Genesis 1); animals had to be at least seven days old to be used for sacrifice (Exodus 22:30); Naaman bathed seven times in the Jordan (2 Kings 5:10); Joshua marched around Jericho for seven days, marching seven times on the last day (Joshua 6:3–4); there are seven things God hates (Proverbs 6:16); Jesus says we are to forgive seventy times seven (Matthew 18:22); and Jesus tells seven woes to the scribes and Pharisees (Matthew 23).

While change has created many new landscapes, not all are pretty to look at. For instance, radical feminism washed in and weakened the solid terrain of traditional gender roles. Sixty-three genders washed in and muddied our common sense. School violence washed in and eroded the innocence of going to school. As the scenery changes as fast as real-time, do we have a crag of constancy somewhere? Is there a mountain we can stand upon that won't be taken by the sea, no matter how hard the thundering rollers of revolution beat upon it? Or will the sand keep giving way when the surf says so?

Revelation 1:4 gives us the answer.

ADDRESSING CHURCHES IN EVERY AGE

Here, we find a community of believers, seven churches in Asia Minor (modern day Turkey), facing opposition from Satan. By addressing *seven* churches, God's Word addresses society's problems that all local churches, in every age, could potentially face. It's a message for the church in general. Although 2,000 years have passed between their society and ours, we face similar satanic opposition as they did, problems of all shapes and sizes. That means that the questions we have about today's society are answered right here. God's Word is our rigid rock that the waves can't break apart and drag out to sea. His will, His ways, and His laws stand forever. And this is what John tells us when he describes God as *"him who is and who was and who is to come"* (ho ōn kai ho ēn kai ho erchomenos).

What's interesting about this phrase is that, in the Greek, it's bad grammar.[2] Did he need writing school? No, actually, John did this on purpose; he *intentionally* made a grammatical error.

John was quoting from Exodus 3:14, which says, "I AM WHO I AM" or *"ho ōn."*[3] In order to make it fit word-perfect into his writing, he had to break with the rules of grammar. While it may not be the best Greek, his readers would recognize that he was referring to the God of the Old Testament. By this, they would understand that the God of the Old Testament is their God, too.

Imagine it like this: after squeezing out a victory in overtime, a football player is interviewed on the field and says, "We done it!" This is incorrect grammar. He should have crowed, "We did it!" But a player short of breath and coming off an adrenaline-filled game isn't intent on using proper grammar. When people read the incorrect grammar in the newspaper, it will evoke a better sense of reality than if an editor fixes the quote.

The incorrect grammar John uses captures the allusion to Exodus 3:14 and makes a *big* statement: the God of the New Testament is the God of the Old Testament—He hasn't changed! How could He? He is perfect in all of His ways. Therefore, he will remain the same, all the way into the twenty-first century—and beyond.

Just because society is evolving doesn't mean God's will and ways change. They don't. When society comes up with something new to say about sexuality, gender roles, family structure, human relationships, good and evil…you can trust that God's Word hasn't bent. God is still holy and He still invites us to be holy, just like Him. (See 1 Peter 1:16.)

This week, remember that Jesus said if you build your house on His Word, you are building your life on a rock. (See Matthew 7:24–27.) Your life will be more resolute and purposeful if you build your life on what God's Word says rather than on the ever-changing fads in ideology and opinion. Don't buy into what "the experts" say. You know the expert: the unchanging God of the Bible.

PRAYER FOR THE WEEK

Dear Heavenly Father—
You are unchanging because You are perfect in all Your ways. This week, I make the decision to put Your Word and ways above anything society has to say. Holy Spirit, fill my heart with understanding from Your Word so that every lie in our culture may be exposed. Because I walk in Your unchanging truth, Your purpose will endure in my life. In Jesus's name, amen!

ACTIVITY FOR THE WEEK

In your prayer journal, write down four or five popular ideas in culture that are contrary to God's Word. Find two or three Scriptures that address these issues and place them next to the respective ideas in your list.

SCRIPTURES FOR THE WEEK

Isaiah 40:8 Hebrews 13:8

Malachi 3:6 James 1:17

Mark 13:31 Revelation 22:18–19

PART II

THE CHURCH AT EPHESUS—
STUDIES ON LOVE

2

DON'T LET GO OF
YOUR CHURCH

*To the angel of the church in Ephesus write: The words of him
who holds the seven stars in his right hand, who walks among
the seven golden lampstands.* (Revelation 2:1a)

Τῷ ἀγγέλῳ τῆς ἐν Ἐφέσῳ ἐκκλησίας γράψον Τάδε λέγει
ὁ κρατῶν τοὺς ἑπτὰ ἀστέρας ἐν τῇ δεξιᾷ αὐτοῦ, ὁ περιπατῶν ἐν μέσῳ τῶν ἑπτὰ λυχνιῶν τῶν χρυσῶν.
(ΑΠΟΚΑΛΥΨΙΣ ΙΩΑΝΝΟΥ 2:1a)

Before shaking hands with the new members of his church, my pastor
would say something that would catch them off guard. "No church
is perfect," he'd say. "If this church *were* perfect, it's *no longer* perfect because *you* just joined." Touché. One point for pastor. The local church

is a congregation of imperfect leaders and imperfect members working together to serve a perfect God. It's an easy concept to accept until, of course, *your* time comes and *you* get offended.

When you join a local church—and every believer should, according to Hebrews 10:25—it's important to understand that there will come a time when someone offends you and you'll have to exercise God's love. It might be the pastor. It may be the pastor's wife. Could be another leader. Perhaps a member. Someone is going to do something that jars you, probably sooner rather than later. Maybe you're reading this and your heart is burning with offense worse than your knee burns when you fall off your bike and scrape it against the sidewalk. Offense is like a forest fire: if you don't work to contain it, it will grow in intensity, spread to new places, and consume things most valuable. Sometimes a spark as slight as a misunderstood comment can engulf whole churches in someone's offended fury.

This brings to mind one of the back-up singers who used to attend our church. I appreciated her singing. However, she was serving in other areas and I didn't want to exhaust her. I called her one day and told her how much I enjoyed her vocals, that she sang well, and that I didn't want to wear her out. I thought she would be happy and feel I was being considerate (that was certainly my heart). I should have known better: never, ever, ever, ever, cut off a musician. She got upset, told everyone I didn't like her singing, got angry at the other singers, and ended up leaving the church…but not before she caused other problems. Until then, I hadn't had any problems with her. A spark, turned forest fire, turned destruction at the church.

Revelation 2:1 sheds some light on the imperfect condition of our local churches and teaches us what our attitude should be in response to it. Here, Jesus is preparing to address the seven most prominent churches in Asia Minor, all of which are far from perfect. (If these seven churches had issues, you can rest assured that other churches back then had issues and that our churches have issues today.) Their problems included false doctrine, sexual immorality, losing love for one another, the love of money, and everything else in between. Before correcting them, Jesus says something that we should not overlook: *"The words of him who holds the seven stars in his right hand."* The seven stars symbolize the pastors of the seven churches.

Because pastors represent their churches, the idea is that Jesus is holding the pastor, the congregation, and everything else in His right hand.

WE ARE SECURE IN CHRIST'S GRASP

Here, the Greek word for "holds" is *kratōn*. This doesn't just mean to casually hold something in your hand, like a can of soda. It means to grip something tightly with power, without any intention of letting it go, because it's irreplaceable, one of a kind, and extremely important. If you fought the crowd in Walmart on Black Friday and grabbed the latest and last game console, despite other bloodthirsty shoppers, it might be a good idea to grip it as hard as you can on your flight to the register. That's the idea. Jesus is clutching these imperfect churches as securely as He can. He has no intention of throwing them aside and letting them go. They are valuable, irreplaceable, and one-of-a-kind, imperfections and all.

> *Kratos* is found in the English word "democracy" (*demos* meaning "*people*" and *kratos* meaning "*power*"). In a democracy, the people hold the power.

Usually, the word that appears after *kratōn* is found in a grammatical case that implies that you are holding only a part of that thing.[4] Think how you hold a mug when you drink your morning coffee. Likely, you only hold it by the handle. You are holding it, but only by part of it.

This isn't how Jesus is gripping the seven churches. We know this because the words that follow *kraton* (*tous hepta asteras*, the seven stars) are found in a case that implies that the *entirety* of the seven churches is being held in Christ's hand.[5] He isn't just hanging onto them. They are clenched within His grip, covered on every side, sheltered in His strong hand.

Before correcting the churches and bringing up their shortcomings, Jesus affirms His love for them. He shows them unconditional love even though they have disappointed Him. He affirms that He won't let go of them until they become everything He desires them to be. Right off the bat, He lets the churches know that He intends to work with them instead of walking away. Sure, Jesus could have hollered at them and dismissed them once and for all. But Christ's love goes deeper than that. God works with those who offend Him; He is patient with those who make mistakes. He expects the same from us.

Has your church demonstrated its shortcomings in front of you lately? Were you quick to be offended? Did you start talking cruelly about those who did you wrong? Maybe you left without ever telling anyone and refuse to go back. If that's the case, this is the week to make things right. Why not change your course and be like Jesus? Extend forgiveness toward your church and be patient with your leaders. Jesus didn't let go of the church and neither should we.

PRAYER FOR THE WEEK

Dear Heavenly Father—
I thank You for my church and for the leaders You've placed over me.
Lord, I am sorry for being offended at my church or those in my church.
I ask You to forgive every wrong word I've spoken and every wrong
measure I have taken. This week, I commit to being like Jesus: to hold
on to my church in prayer until it becomes everything You desire it to
be. I will walk in love with my church and get along with those there.
And I refuse to leave my church, offended. I am a blessing to my church
and my church is a blessing to me. In Jesus's name, amen!

ACTIVITY FOR THE WEEK

In your prayer journal, list five things about your church that are wonderful and have helped you grow in Christ. Next, list five things about your pastor and leadership that are wonderful and have helped you grow. Spend the week thanking God for these ten things and, at the end of the week, record in your prayer journal how this has changed your heart toward your church.

SCRIPTURES FOR THE WEEK

Proverbs 10:12   Hebrews 10:24–25

1 Timothy 3:14–15   Hebrews 13:7

1 Timothy 5:17–19   Hebrews 13:17

3

YOUR PASSPORT IS ALL YOU NEED

...Who walks among the seven golden lampstands.
(Revelation 2:1b)

...ὁ περιπατῶν ἐν μέσῳ τῶν ἑπτὰ λυχνιῶν τῶν χρυσῶν.
(ΑΠΟΚΑΛΥΨΙΣ ΙΩΑΝΝΟΥ 2:1b)

Your passport is the only thing you *need* to travel the world. You don't need an entire suitcase just for shoes. You can leave your Hawaiian shirt collection in your closet. Toiletries? Many third-world countries have a selection of toothpaste. The only thing the Transportation Security Administration cares about is whether you have that cardboard profile with your mugshot slapped on it. If you don't, you're looking at a vacation in the backyard.

While you're away, if you don't guard your passport really well, you may end up adding a visit to the embassy before you get home.

I've lost just about everything on trips, including money, credit cards, watches—I've even lost my prescription eyeglass three times: once in Malta, once in Sicily, and once in Malaysia. (I finally had to get LASIK.) I've never lost my passport, though. I treat it like it's one of my appendages. It stays with me at all times, in all places. When I walk out of my hotel room in the morning, I tap my front right pants pocket to make sure it's there. All throughout the day I give my pocket little pats so I know it's doing well. And when I go to bed, I place it on my nightstand next to my head. My passport gets the royal treatment. If I have it, I can continue traveling.

WE CAN'T LIVE WITHOUT JESUS

In Revelation 2:1b, we discover that the presence of Jesus is the one exclusive and essential thing that our Christian lives need and cannot continue without. It enables a church to be a church and a Christian to serve the kingdom of God. Therefore, we must give it the royal treatment. We need to make sure it goes with us out the door in the morning, stays with us during the day, and is beside us when we doze off to sleep at night.

In this verse, the seven churches of Asia Minor are referred to as lampstands. The Greek word for "lampstand" is *lychnia*. Think of a Jewish menorah: a base made from gold and seven places for a lamp.[6] In the Old Testament, a lampstand represented the presence of God, which was the source of Israel's might. When Israel faced resistance rebuilding its temple, Zechariah reminded them that it was the Spirit of God that would empower them. Military might, human expertise, and manpower were insufficient. The task required the presence of the Spirit of God—the same Spirit that delivered the children of Israel out of Egypt with many mighty miracles. (See 2 Kings 17:36.) The lampstand in Zechariah's vision served as this reminder. (See Zechariah 4:2–6.)

A "lychnis" is a genus that comprises several types of flowers native to Europe, Asia, and Africa. This comes from *lychnos*, the Greek word for "lamp." It's thought that the leaves of these flowers were

A lampstand also stood in the holy place in the tabernacle of Moses. (See Exodus 25:31.) The light that emanated from it characterized the holy, life-giving power of God that came from being near His presence. The lampstand represents a connection between the power of God and the presence of God. If we want power in our lives, the *one* thing we need is the presence. There are some doors our college degrees can't open. There are some problems our intellectual proficiency can't solve. And you can be certain there are some challenges our own strength can't match. But these are no contest for God's presence.

The next thing that demonstrates the primacy of God's presence is that this verse refers to Jesus as He *"who walks among"* the seven churches. The Greek word for "walks" is *peripateō*. This word means to walk to-and-fro and go here-and-there. It indicates busyness and activity. We find it in a tense that refers to action happening continuously, unceasingly, and without any interruption.[7] It gives us a picture of the intimate, ongoing presence of Jesus within the lives of His churches. He's invited among them and is busy accomplishing His ministry through the Holy Spirit. He's calling to sinners, healing the sick, comforting the bereaved, encouraging the broken, and giving hope to those who've lost meaning in this life. The will of God for the local church and for our own personal lives is for Jesus to walk to-and-fro among us and accompany us with His uninterrupted presence.

This week, remember that the presence of Jesus isn't *a part* of your life, it *is* your life. His presence is the enabling power you need to be a godly husband or wife. It's the secret to being an effective pastor and minister. It's the vigor it takes to be successful in business. When Jesus is walking among your endeavors, they'll be full of life and success. All you have to do is make sure the presence stays with you. Stay mindful of it, rejoice that is with you, and don't let anything near it that might put it at risk. Remember, it's your passport—it's all you need.

PRAYER FOR THE WEEK

Dear Heavenly Father—
This week, I invite the presence of the Lord Jesus into my life and into
everything I am involved in for the kingdom. May Your Spirit fill me
fresh and empower me. May the Lord Jesus work through me to ac-
complish His work here on the earth. Lord Jesus, may all those I en-
counter this week feel Your tangible presence and may their lives be
transformed because of it. In Jesus's name, amen!

ACTIVITY FOR THE WEEK

Is there an area of your life that needs a fresh encounter with the presence of God? Make a list of things that you would like God to anoint anew
with His presence. Pick a time when you can consistently seek God each
day this week. During these times of prayer, call out to God and ask Him
to fill these areas of your life with His presence.

SCRIPTURES FOR THE WEEK

Exodus 33:14	Psalm 31:20
Psalm 16:11	Psalm 84:10
Psalm 23:6	John 14:16–17

4

GOD, OUR PHOTOGRAPHER

I know your works...   (Revelation 2:2a)

Οἶδα τὰ ἔργα...   (ΑΠΟΚΑΛΥΨΙΣ ΙΩΑΝΝΟΥ 2:2a)

Google Earth is amazing. I can't think of a better way to waste time. Who doesn't enjoy taking a few hours to look for creepy abnormalities hidden around our planet? If you don't know how it works, have no fear. You can just google "strange things found on Google Earth" and you'll be off to the races. We're talking shipwrecks, remote pyramids, and some hair-raising things you can discover for yourself. You'll have a bird's eye view of it all.

Google Earth Street View came along in 2008 and took things to the next level. This sophisticated technology provides 360-degree, panoramic, street-level views, allowing users to see everything at ground level. Looking to plan a date? No problem. Scope out restaurants as if you were in front of them. Websites can't fool anyone anymore. If the place is a pigsty, Google Street View will let you know. You can also look at your house, your boss's house, and the house of your high school crush who dumped you twenty-five years ago.

Google gets its panoramic images from the cameras they mount on the Google car. It drives up and down its route, scanning, measuring, and taking pictures. Have you ever seen one driving by? I have. I usually wave, hoping I'll show up on their updated maps. Just remember, Google is among you and is able to see exactly what you're doing. It has an intimate knowledge of the whole world.

> The word "photograph" comes from two Greek words: *phōs* meaning "light" and *graphe* meaning "drawing." A photograph is a drawing made by light.

In Revelation 2:2, Jesus tells the church in Ephesus something intimate—Google Street View intimate. He says, *"I know your works"* (*Oida ta erga sou*). Four words that don't seem like much, but in the Greek, they pack a punch. The first thing to note is that Jesus uses the word *oida*. There are a couple other words that can be translated "to know" (*ginōskō, epistamai*) but Jesus chose the one that expresses *total, comprehensive knowledge.* It is intimate knowledge that comes from being up close and personal. This knowledge isn't hazy on the details. It doesn't struggle to remember. It preserves the particulars. In the mind's eye, everything is sharp and clear, like a well-taken photograph.

Next, we find *oida* in a tense that expresses a past event that has present consequences.[8] In other words, Christ's comprehensive and photographic knowledge of the church in Ephesus is the result of His previous action—walking among them and being in their presence (verse 2:1b). Like a Google car with a highly sophisticated camera mounted on top, Jesus moved up and down the church in Ephesus, recording every fine detail. He logged their activity as a congregation and as individuals. He even noted *why* they did what they did. Jesus had photographed all of the facts and had a standing archive of truth. This means that He saw the good, the bad, *and* the ugly, just as Google Earth captures the beauty of the terrain in places mankind has never set foot, but also captures men coming out of unsavory clubs and people brawling on the street.

The Ephesians, like any of us, would have had mixed feelings about this. On one hand, they would have felt vindicated: all of their unnoticed good works had been recorded by the One who gives out the eternal rewards. On the other hand, everything they thought they had gotten away with had also been seen by the same judge.

JESUS KNOWS EVERYTHING WE DO

Christ wants us to know that intimacy with Him comes with His superior knowledge of everything we do and why we do it. He won't overlook anything we do in service to Him but He won't turn a blind eye to those things that displease Him. He is a holy God who wants us to draw closer to Him. For that to be possible, He has to point out the areas in our life we need to correct.

This week, remember that Christ is driving up and down your life measuring, scanning, and collecting data. If someone has unjustly accused you of something you didn't do, don't fret. Seriously. Stop trying to defend yourself and remember it's on film in Christ's archives. He will make it right. If you've been serving your church and are feeling a little down because nobody has commended you, lift that chin and rejoice. God has seen the sacrifices you've made for the children's Bible school, the youth group, the cleaning crew, the evangelism team, and all of the other groups helping out. Your reward is coming.

And if you've done something you shouldn't have or if you've been doing something shameful in secret, God's mercy is drawing you to repent and get things right with Him. Instead of running or hiding, why not use this moment to receive God's grace and forgiveness? It's a new day to start fresh. The Google Car is out here to make life better. Will you take advantage of it?

PRAYER FOR THE WEEK

Dear Heavenly Father—
It is my desire to be close to You. I know that You see all and know all about my life; nothing escapes Your sight. I also know that You are just and merciful, so I will not worry over the situations where I've been

*treated unfairly or undeservingly. I also ask You to forgive me for those
things I've done to displease You. I take responsibility for them and ask
You for Your grace and the power of the Holy Spirit to overcome them.
May everything You see me do this week bring You glory. In Jesus's
name, amen!*

ACTIVITY FOR THE WEEK

Put a picture of the Google car on your phone's home screen. Let it
serve as a reminder, every time you look at your phone, that God is keeping
a meticulous eye on each event that takes place in your life. This should
encourage you and also inspire you to give God your best, every second of
the day.

SCRIPTURES FOR THE WEEK

2 Chronicles 16:9   Zechariah 4:10

Job 31:4   Hebrews 4:13

Jeremiah 16:17   1 John 3:20

5

THE ONE INGREDIENT YOU CAN'T DO WITHOUT

But I have this against you, that you have abandoned the love you had at first. Remember therefore from where you have fallen; repent, and do the works you did at first.

(Revelation 2:4–5a)

ἀλλ' ἔχω κατὰ σοῦ ὅτι τὴν ἀγάπην σου τὴν πρώτην ἀφῆκες. μνημόνευε οὖν πόθεν πέπτωκας καὶ μετανόησον καὶ τὰ πρῶτα ἔργα ποίησον.

(ΑΠΟΚΑΛΥΨΙΣ ΙΩΑΝΝΟΥ 2:4–5a)

One missing ingredient can ruin the entire entree. Just ask my pal, Josh. Josh had just gone through a Western movie phase and began to think he was John Wayne, the Duke, the new tough guy in town who was done eating his mother's tuna salad sandwiches. It was time for him to put some punch in his reputation and concoct his own hard-hitting chili. After hours of throwing this and that into his bubbling pot, Josh let us have the first taste. As we sent the chili back and forth from cheek to cheek, it became apparent something wasn't right. It lacked the *bang* that puts hair on your chest. I was ready for a tuna salad sandwich.

Seeing our confusion, the Duke's mother yanked the spoon from my hand and gave it a go. With a maternal roll of the eyes, she told her son, "I'm sorry to inform you, Mr. Wayne, but you forgot to add the chili powder." It's the one thing that makes chili, chili, and it didn't find its way into the pot. It didn't matter that filet mignon was espousing its flavors to the succulent vegetables—it was good for nothing because the missing ingredient wasn't present to pull it all together. Way to go, Duke!

The Ephesian church, too, learned a lesson about missing ingredients. Of the seven churches listed in Revelation, Ephesus was the premier. That's why it's listed first. Part of its greatness had to do with where it was located. Ephesus was the greatest city in all of Asia at the time. It boasted the greatest harbor and market place in that region of the world. Cultures, customs, and religion met in Ephesus. One Roman writer called Ephesus the "Light of Asia" because it shone with greatness. When the Christian church showed up in Ephesus, it did so with a bang that was brighter.

The Ephesian church had a mighty beginning: Paul started it (see Acts 18:19) and some of Christianity's strongest leaders had been associated with it, including Timothy, Aquila, Priscilla, and Apollos. Here, Christianity experienced some of its first great victories: people were baptized in the Spirit (see Acts 19:1–7), the whole city experienced revival (see Acts 19:9–10), witchcraft was defeated (see Acts 19:19–20), and powerful miracles occurred (see Acts 19:16).

Its legacy was the foundation of its superb stature. Jesus said the church had many of the right ingredients: it worked hard, endured much, and defended itself from false teachers who came to destroy it from the inside out. Notice:

> *I know your works, your toil and your patient endurance, and how*
> *you cannot bear with those who are evil, but have tested those who call*

themselves apostles and are not, and found them to be false.

(Revelation 2:2)

> Kopophobia (*Kopos* meaning "weary" and *phobos* meaning "fear")
> is an abnormal fear of being tired or fatigued. Those affected may
> avoid activity to the detriment of their personal and professional
> lives. They may go to bed early to avoid being tired when they wake
> up the next day.

The Greek word for "toil," *kopos*, is no small word. It means "to be weary from taking a beating." It describes the most intense and strenuous of labor, like a soldier in battle, a wrestler engaged in competition, or a messenger who has run long to deliver an important letter. No church worked as vigorously as the Ephesians.

The Ephesians also had patient endurance. The Greek word for "patient endurance," *hypomonē*, didn't just mean waiting in a traffic jam without a fuss. It was the kind of gallantry that withstood hazard until the situation had turned into victory. The Ephesian church had overcome decades of threats, grown holy in the midst of wicked society, and had expanded despite the pushback from the powers of darkness. (See Ephesians 6:10–12.) It knew something about the glory of God.

On top of that, the church had preserved the pure doctrine of God's Word by detecting and removing false teachers from their assembly. The Greek word "tested," *peirazō*, was used to describe assessing a city—finding out what it's made of—to see if could be conquered. The Ephesians stood up to bullies and protected their turf.

A KEY INGREDIENT WAS MISSING

Despite these wonderful ingredients, the chili powder was missing. This was none other than love. The Ephesian church had grown cold and it was rare to find them showing God's love to one other within their community. This was a big problem. Love comes from God (see Romans 5:8), is evidence of eternal life (see 1 John 3:14), and demonstrates to the world that we are followers of Christ (see John 13:35). This is why it is the essential ingredient that we can't leave out. And Jesus didn't find a drop of it in the Ephesian church. That's why He was so upset.

But the Lord told them how to add it in. First, they were to "remember" from where they had fallen or remember when love was abundant among them. The Greek word for "remember," *mnēmoneuō*, is found in a tense that implies a continual remembering.[9] They were supposed to think, over and over again, about the way things were when their community was saturated with God's love.

Next, they were to repent. The Greek word for "repent," *metanoeō*, is used twice in verse 5 to emphasize how important repentance was to restoring God's love back into their community. It is found in a tense that emphasizes that their repentance was to be completed *at once*.[10] The Ephesians were to make an immediate, decisive decision to humble themselves before God and fix the problem. To accomplish this, Jesus tells them, *"Do the works you did at first"*—that is, show each other the love they once had for one another. The Greek word for "do," *poieō*, is also found in the same tense as repent (*metanoeō*), meaning they were not to wait to act. Love was to start *now*.

Like the Ephesians, we may end up accomplishing titanic achievements for the kingdom of God: we may build a booming ministry, earn a high education, travel to many foreign lands, and be on the cusp of the move of God. But if we neglect love, God won't be pleased, because love is what makes everything else pleasant to His taste. So, this week, go after kingdom feats with all your might. Just make sure to add the love.

PRAYER FOR THE WEEK

Dear Heavenly Father—
I thank You that the moment I was saved, You placed Your love in my heart through the Holy Spirit. You have asked me to share this love with those around me. This is high priority to You so it's a high priority to me. Holy Spirit, show me how to love when it's hard, and give me special opportunities to share this love with those who have yet to know You. I commit myself to Your love, no matter what I set my hands to do. In Jesus's name, amen!

ACTIVITY FOR THE WEEK

Consider the accomplishments you are proudest of. Have these, in any way, affected the way you show love to God's people? If yes, how so? Journal about it.

SCRIPTURES FOR THE WEEK

Proverbs 10:12

1 Corinthians 13:4–8

1 Corinthians 16:14

Colossians 3:14

1 John 4:8

1 Peter 4:8

6

#LOVEWARNS

If not, I will come to you and remove your lampstand from its place, unless you repent. (Revelation 2:5b)

εἰ δὲ μή, ἔρχομαί σοι καὶ κινήσω τὴν λυχνίαν σου ἐκ τοῦ τόπου αὐτῆς, ἐὰν μὴ μετανοήσῃς.

(ΑΠΟΚΑΛΥΨΙΣ ΙΩΑΝΝΟΥ 2:5b)

Cyberspace is a vast buffet table of information, time is our plate, and we earthlings want to cram as much onto it as we can. So, we look for tidbits—small pieces of information—that tell us everything we need to hear...or think we need to hear. No way are we watching the whole interview. Just show us the part where the politician fumbles his words and ruins his chance for reelection.

Online news sources have figured this out. To accommodate their readers, they now summarize their article in bullet points at the top, before the article even begins. I'll glance at them and *if* something strikes me, I *may* skim the article.

If content providers don't do things in bits, consequences will include no views, no shares, or the dreaded thumbs down (well, at least someone *attempted* to watch it). No one is interested in a 16:00 YouTube video unless it's a celebrity, essential information, or someone doing something to ruin themselves.

Living in an information bit world has had its consequences. People engage with content when it appeals to what they like, as proved by the "like." Content providers know this and create their information to fit people's preferences. Find the popular accounts on social media. Most of them are slogans that inspire, encourage, and create a sense of acceptance within their followers. There's nothing wrong with this, so long as we don't stop here. But unfortunately, it happens too often. As a result, we end up with a culture preoccupied with slogans rather than being set on serious engagement with God's Word.

One such bit-sized slogan that has made its way onto T-shirts, bumper stickers, and people's social profiles is "Love Wins." It's become the call-to-arms for those demanding tolerance toward alternative lifestyles. It's a call for acceptance and a notice that anything short of it will incur backlash—like posts being trolled, expulsion from school, or intense debate during Thanksgiving dinner.

Idioms are words and phrases that mean something different than their literal meaning—for example, "out of shape" and "beat around the bush." In order to understand and use idioms, one must familiarize themselves with the language's culture. Learning biblical customs goes "hand in glove" with learning Koine Greek.

GOD'S LOVE WARNS US

Let's forget the slogan for a second and engage with God's Word. Revelation 2:5 tells us something interesting about God's love: it warns. After commanding the Ephesians to repent for their lack of love toward one another, Jesus gives them an ultimatum. He begins it by saying, "If not" (*ei de mē*). In Greek, this is a strong idiom that can also be translated "otherwise, but if not." Its purpose is to introduce what will happen to the Ephesians if they decide not to repent for their loveless community. *But if not.* The consequences Jesus is about to present will only occur *if* His conditions aren't met. God thinks the Ephesians need to repent, *but* if they don't think they do, they're headed for trouble. Finally, there is the negative particle, *mē*, the negative that's always used when a condition isn't met. Assuming the Ephesians are *not* going to comply, they're looking at punishment.

The punishment is strong. Jesus says, *"I will come to you and remove your lampstand from its place."* The Greek word for "I will come" is *erchomai*. It's actually found here in the present tense and is best translated, "I am coming." The use of the present tense is to dramatize just how close Christ was to punishing the church. He has momentum, moving with speed, right there, one step away from removing His presence and power from their lives. Does this sound like a loving God? When you consider everything, it certainly does.

While God is slow to anger (see Psalm 103:8), He is holy and there comes a time when He must deal with sin. His holiness demands it. But the very fact that Jesus slowed His momentum to give the church one *final* warning shows that God's heart is really *for* us. He wants our best. He doesn't want to punish us, but He can't let us get away with sin either. From this, we see that God's love isn't just mawkish tolerance. It's a perfect balance between patience for those who fall short and discipline for those who refuse His grace. Unfortunately, bits about discipline don't go over well with people; it chafes their agenda—and it certainly doesn't perform well on social media. And so, we're left with a culture that doesn't think it needs to heed God's warnings to win.

There's a lot of love in a warning, especially God's. Don't misconstrue Him or take Him the wrong way; He just wants the best for you. Has He been warning you about anything lately? He must love you a lot. Why not respond to His warning this week? Re-think. Shift your course, change your actions, and experience the mercy and grace of God, who is on your side. (See Romans 8:31.)

PRAYER FOR THE WEEK

Dear Heavenly Father—
You love me so much that You warn me when I'm in trouble, and call
to me when I'm headed for danger. Thank You for not just leaving me
be. I humble myself and take heed to Your warnings. I will do exactly
what You ask, right away. May I continue to experience Your love and
hear Your guiding voice this week. In Jesus's name, amen!

ACTIVITY FOR THE WEEK

Take an inventory: make a list of things God has been warning you
about. What is the warning? Why do you think He is warning you about
that? How will heeding His warning improve your relationship with Him
and with other people? Does His warning reveal to you all the more how
much He loves you?

SCRIPTURES FOR THE WEEK

Deuteronomy 8:5   Proverbs 13:24

Psalm 94:12   Hebrews 12:5–6

Proverbs 3:12   Revelation 3:19

7

WILL YOU JOIN GOD IN HIS HATE?

Yet this you have: you hate the works of the Nicolaitans, which I also hate. (Revelation 2:6)

ἀλλὰ τοῦτο ἔχεις, ὅτι μισεῖς τὰ ἔργα τῶν Νικολαϊτῶν ἃ κἀγὼ μισῶ. (ΑΠΟΚΑΛΥΨΙΣ ΙΩΑΝΝΟΥ 2:6)

A Twitter storm erupts whenever pop culture puts on a spectacle. The Oscars, the Grammys, the Super Bowl halftime event—they spin up a vortex of hashtags and memes that sail across our screens for days, if not weeks. There's always that Category 5 hurricane—you know, that one outfit or performance that rips up what we hold sacred and sends it sailing onto its head in the name of "art," "progress," and "being with the times." You can expect applause from those who don't know Christ. But what about the singer on the worship team who is retweeting, liking, and sharing their approval?

In Revelation 2:6, Jesus gives us a lesson on love that we need to be reminded of as often as possible today. Loving God means hating what He hates—*not* liking, reposting, or sharing with your friends. It's interesting that Jesus brings up hatred immediately after He rebukes the Ephesians for their lack of love. The first thing He says is, "*Yet*" (*alla*). Its placement right after Christ's rebuke to the Ephesians makes it come off quite strong. Imagine a coach telling a basketball team, "You missed all your free throws, didn't get back on defense, and you hardly rebounded, and so you'll be getting extra laps at practice next week. *Yet* you did manage to win the game and I'm happy about that." Although the Ephesians had made a mistake worthy of discipline, Christ still had something to commend them for.

Next, Jesus says, "*This you have*" (*touto echeis*). *Touto* (this) and *echeis* (you have) are a special combination of words that imply having "favor" or "advantage." Despite all of their issues, the Ephesians still had favor with God. What gave them that favor? They hated the works of the Nicolaitans.

IT'S AN INTENSE HATRED

Before we find out who the Nicolaitans are and what they were doing, we need to understand the word for "hate." The Greek verb is *miseō*. It's stronger than our English word "hate." Today, we often say we hate things when we just don't like them: "I hate carbs," "I hate gluten," "I hate slow streaming 3G." If it really came down to it, though, you'd probably eat bread if you had nothing else to eat and 3G is better than no G. Here, *miseō* means to detest something so strongly there is no tolerance for it. It means to have no regard and ability to bear with something. It's more like the way you feel about tarantulas, king cobras, and infomercials.

What's interesting is that Jesus says this hatred formed a bond between Him and the Ephesian church. This is found in the words "*I also hate.*" "I also" is just one word in the Greek, *kagō*. It is a combination of *kai* (and, even, also) and *egō* (I), meaning literally "even I" or "also I." Jesus is saying, "You hate what they are doing, and I also hate what they are doing. Together, we hate what they are doing!" Together, they stood united in hatred against the works of the Nicolaitans. This is a unique lesson. Today's culture teaches that tolerance in the name of love makes us stand with God, but here, Jesus says hatred of evil in the name of love gives us a place of favor with Him.

> Along with the Great Pyramid of Giza and the Lighthouse of Alexandria, the Temple of Artemis is among the Seven Wonders of the Ancient World.

Now, to the Nicolaitans. These were the reformist religious people of the day. Their leader, Nicolaus, is mentioned in Acts 6:5 as being among the seven original deacons. Nicolaus veered from the truth by teaching loose living and unrestraint toward pleasure. He didn't think he was destroying Christianity, but improving it. (Have you ever heard that one before?) Ephesus was a culture filled with idolatry and the location of the temple of Artemis, "the great mother goddess" of fertility, where thousands of her priests served. Nicolaus began bending under the weight of the culture and felt that Christianity should find a place of compromise with the world and dabble in idol worship. He probably wondered what the big deal was. Maybe he felt he saw good in the idol worshippers. Perhaps he felt the Christians were being too tough on them.

Church history teaches that Nicolaus began teaching: 1) the law has come to an end and we have more liberty to do what we want; 2) the body is evil so it's inconsequential what we do with it; and 3) we have grace, so no need to be concerned about punishment. Does any of this sound familiar today? Christ commended the Ephesians for joining with Him in His *hatred* toward these notions. Their abhorrence of Nicolaus's teachings kept the world from corrupting the church and enabled the church to continue transforming the world.

If we're serious about loving God, we must seek Him for a heart to hate what He hates. (See Psalm 36:2–4.) We do no service to the kingdom by buddying-up with the culture. This week, make a decision that you are going to hate the works of the Nicolaitans. The more you hate evil, the more God's love will fill your heart for those ensnared in it. This will give you favor and power with God.

PRAYER FOR THE WEEK

Dear Heavenly Father—
I realize that loving with all my heart means feeling the way You feel
about things. Place in my heart an abhorrence for sin and wickedness.
May my philosophy, my worldview, and my lifestyle all reflect my love
of Your truth. Holy Spirit, fill my heart with mercy and compassion for
those who are trapped in wickedness. May I never be condemning and
self-righteous. Rather, may I be filled with Your power to deliver them
and show them the truth. In Jesus's name, amen!

ACTIVITY FOR THE WEEK

Clean up your social media. Unfollow trash accounts, undo retweets
that don't please the Lord, and delete posts that don't represent your hatred
for evil. In their place, follow accounts that are edifying and display love for
God's truth.

SCRIPTURES FOR THE WEEK

Psalm 45:7	Amos 5:5
Psalm 97:10	Romans 12:9
Proverbs 8:13	Hebrews 1:9

8

HEARING GOD'S VOICE IS A HIGH PRIORITY

He who has an ear, let him hear what the Spirit says to the churches. (Revelation 2:7a)

ὁ ἔχων οὖς ἀκουσάτω τί τὸ πνεῦμα λέγει ταῖς ἐκκλησί-
αις. (ΑΠΟΚΑΛΥΨΙΣ ΙΩΑΝΝΟΥ 2:7a)

What would happen if you spent a whole Saturday afternoon around the house pretending not to hear your spouse? "Honey, can you turn the TV down?" No answer. "Sweetheart, where are my polka dot socks?" Silence. "Babe, want to go for fro-yo later?" I'm guessing someone is going to end up sleeping on the couch or checking into the Comfort Suites.

Happy relationships are built on successful communication, which includes effective listening. An intimate walk with Christ is no different. To be near Christ, we must hear His Spirit. In fact, your relationship with God began when you heard His Spirit for the first time. There you were, in a pitiful state of living, when Spirit's voice boomed like thunder and sent shockwaves of conviction through your soul. He called you out of darkness and into His marvelous light. (See 1 Peter 2:9.) Your new life was born.

God doesn't give us the silent treatment after we hear Him. He doesn't think, *Well, I hope they enjoyed hearing My voice because they won't hear it again until they get to heaven.* He intends to speak to us consistently throughout this life. He calls us His sons and daughters. (See 2 Corinthians 6:18.) There's a nearness that comes with that, expressed through faithful communication.

A woman once asked me why God never speaks to her. My sarcastic side wanted to tell her, "He probably doesn't like you." It sounds mean and it's definitely *not* true. But it's what she was implying. How do I know? Because the next thing she said was, "He doesn't like me." This precious sister believed that God plays favorites. God's word is clear that he doesn't. (See Romans 2:11). God desires to speak to all of His children, including you. If there is anything He makes clear in Revelation, it's this.

GOD DRIVES HOME HIS POINT

In Revelation 2:7, we find a phrase that is used not just once, not twice, but seven times in two chapters: *"He who has an ear, let him hear what the Spirit says to the churches"* (ho echon ous akousatō ti to pneuma legei tais ek-klēsiais). It's God's Word because God said it once. But repeating it seven times in two chapters emphasizes just how much God wants us to understand this.

It's like driving in the car with my seven-year-old nephew. "Uncle, I have to use the bathroom." At this point, I'm thinking, *well, we'll need to gas up in about an hour so we'll stop then.* But if he says it again, I know I should start looking for a stop *now.* And if he says it five more times after that, I'd better find a police escort. His need to use the bathroom suddenly becomes high priority.

"Acoustic" comes from the Greek word family wherein *akouō* belongs. "Acoustics" refer to sound properties, such as an "acoustic" guitar or the "acoustics" of a room.

Hearing God's voice is a high priority for all of us. This is emphasized by the fact that Christ says, *"Let him hear."* Here, we find the verb "to hear" (*akouō*) functioning in a way that makes hearing God a high priority.[11] It could be translated, "I command you to hear!" or "You must hear!" It's like my nephew saying, "Uncle, pull over! I need to go! Pull over now!" We don't have an option if we want intimacy with God; we *need* to hear His voice.

His voice is possible for all of us to hear. This is demonstrated by the fact that Christ addresses the "churches" (*ekklesiais*). The use of the plural tells us that the Spirit doesn't *just* speak to the Ephesian church or the other six churches. He speaks to everyone—you, me, and people in faraway places. God speaks to *all of us* because He wants to be close to His creation.

This is further confirmed by the term, *"He who has an ear"* (*ho echon ous*). This is an idiom. "Having an ear" means being able to hear. It means that people within His churches should be able to hear Him. There's no indicting God. He tells us seven times that He is speaking to every last one of us.

If your intimacy with the Lord has been obstructed because you haven't been able to hear God's voice, it's not because God isn't speaking to you. Instead of blaming God, why not ask the Holy Spirit why you've been unable to hear His sweet, gentle voice. Have you been too busy with work? Do you spend a lot of time worrying? Worrying will blare out God's still, small voice. How's your prayer life? Are you praying in the Spirit and seeking God until He fills you with a new word for today?

Go forward into this week confident that God has a word for you. Then, set yourself up to hear that word. That may mean listening to sermons on the treadmill instead of your cardio playlist. It could mean getting up an extra half hour early to worship. And it might even mean going to church on Sundays *and* Wednesdays. It'll be worth it when God speaks. You'll realize that God has created you to hear His voice. Nothing in our busy lives tops that kind of intimacy with God.

PRAYER FOR THE WEEK

Dear Heavenly Father—
You have created me to hear Your voice. It is Your desire that I walk near You and beside You. This week, I adjust my ears to hear what it is that You want to share with me. Holy Spirit, speak Your words of direction, understanding, wisdom, and knowledge into my life. May I live each day in tune with Your prophetic voice. In Jesus's name, amen!

ACTIVITY FOR THE WEEK

Spend significant time praying in the Spirit this week. This will make you more sensitive to His voice. As the week passes, keep a running list of ways God leads you. Did you experience more leading from God than in weeks prior? What does this tell you about the connection between prayer and hearing God's voice?

SCRIPTURES FOR THE WEEK

Isaiah 6:10	John 10:27
Matthew 13:14–15	John 16:13
John 8:47	1 Timothy 4:1

9

AN INVITATION TO GOD'S GARDEN

To the one who conquers I will grant to eat of the tree of life, which is in the paradise of God. (Revelation 2:7b)

τῷ νικῶντι δώσω αὐτῷ φαγεῖν ἐκ τοῦ ξύλου τῆς ζωῆς, ὅ ἐστιν ἐν τῷ παραδείσῳ τοῦ θεοῦ.
(ΑΠΟΚΑΛΥΨΙΣ ΙΩΑΝΝΟΥ 2:7b)

You could have gotten away with it! If you've ever heard that thought, you've been smacked in the face by the devil. That's what he gives you for resisting a moment of fierce temptation. *You'd still be going to heaven. You'd even be laughing about it now.* This is Satan's way of suggesting to you that sin isn't always a bad idea. He's marinating you in faulty reasoning so he can roast you over the flame of sin the next time he wants to have you for dinner.

One of Satan's lies is that your life isn't as good as those who've enjoyed some sin. *See, they're doing just fine! They are happy, they make more money… their kids are even more successful than yours.* If you listen to these thoughts, you're inevitably going to think that God has let you down. It will suck the joy out of serving His kingdom and will end up leaving you bitter.

JESUS OFFERS ENCOURAGEMENT

In Revelation 2:7, Jesus encourages the Ephesians. He knows they were paying a great price to resist the social pressures of Ephesus. Christ wanted them to know that His rewards are not based on how much we get away with. His rewards are based on being obedient and overcoming the wickedness that is in the world. This is demonstrated by the words *"the one who conquers"* (*tō nikōnti*). They stress continuing, ongoing action that doesn't quit.[12] It could be translated "to the one conquering." It doesn't mean to conquer one time; it means a day-to-day conquering that spans a lifetime: conquering, conquering, and conquering. This continuous conquering means being resolute in the face of Satan's best enticements.

I learned what it meant to be resolute when I watched my friend do the Keto diet. We were in Israel. The days started at the hotel buffet. On day one, I piled pancakes on my plate and drizzled them with dense syrup. He loaded his plate up with crisp greens, sturdy bacon, and fluffy eggs. By 9:30 a.m., I was exhausted. Walking around was more difficult than convincing flat-earth conspirators the planet is round. "It's those carbs you stuffed your face with this morning," my friend said. That did it. I was officially on the Keto diet.

Day two was salad, cucumbers, and lots of bacon. It made a big difference. I was zipping around the holy land like a happy dog at the beach. Then day three came. There I was in line, ready to fuel up on some salad, when I noticed they had broken out the French toast. A spring of saliva burst in my mouth. That's all she wrote. My Keto diet lasted 23 hours and 32 minutes. But not my friend; he didn't eat a single carb. I even dared him to try, but he rejected my offer like I was a robo-caller. He was resolute, staunch, and unyielding in the face of French toast. One good day didn't warrant a day to cheat.

Now, the verb "conquer" (*nikaō*) is of special interest. It comes from the Greek goddess who personified victory, Nike. It means "crushing victory; to overthrow an opposing force; decisive triumph that is seen by every eye." It's not a light win; it's routing victory. Nikes are shoes made for champions who stomp, smash, and smother their opponent in front of the crowd. This is the kind of victory God wants His people to consistently demonstrate over sin.

The most popular statue of Nike, *Winged Victory of Samothrace*, was created in the second century B.C. to commemorate a victorious naval battle. This original marble statue is on display at the Louvre in Paris.

GOD EXPECTS US TO KEEP WINNING

Conquerors never think of taking a loss because they're bored with victory. God addresses "the one who conquers" in His message to each of the seven churches to emphasize that God fully expects His people to keep on winning…and winning and winning.

Here, Christ gives those who consistently conquer sin the special promise of eating from the tree of life in the paradise of God. The word paradise (*paradeisos*) is borrowed from a Persian word (*pairidaeza*). It first referred to the lush gardens of Persian monarchs. They were walled off to shut out the scorching desert. Within, they were enchanting. They contained refreshing canals, exotic flowers, and luscious fruits of all kinds. Here, in Revelation, it describes eternal serenity in the presence of God, walled off from evil and plenteous with every holy delight, including the tree of life.

Eating from the tree of life represents experiencing life how God intended it to be before the fall. This is a vivid picture. It isn't yanking off a hard apple from your grandma's tree. Imagine approaching a sweet-scented sapling, its fruit so succulent that a shake of the stem sends one sailing into your palm. Its juices seep from the skin and your fingers become sticky from the sugary syrup. It tastes like a better world. It's joy under the reign of the Messiah, who puts flavor back into living. It's also the eternal reward for the conquerors who refused to believe that sin ever made them miss a thing.

God has given us an invitation to His garden. He wants to honor us and reward us for overcoming. Don't let Satan bargain you for something cheap. Every resolute stand against temptation is an RSVP to be at the banquet in God's garden. It's going to be a splendid time. It's certainly something to rejoice about this week.

PRAYER FOR THE WEEK

Dear Heavenly Father—
Thank You for giving me victory over sin through the power of Your Holy Spirit and through Your Word. I'll never regret saying no to sin. The hope of a delightful eternity with You far outweighs the fleeting pleasures of carnal gratification. I'm not looking to get away with anything. Instead, I'm RSVP'ing to be with You in paradise. Until then, You have my obedience. In Jesus's name, amen!

ACTIVITY FOR THE WEEK

Instead of focusing on the things you could have gotten away with, fix your attention on unexpected blessings that God has given you. Look back at the last three years. Make a list of seven things God blessed you with that you could have never expected. How is this attached to your obedience? Does God reward the faithful?

SCRIPTURES FOR THE WEEK

John 16:33	1 Corinthians 10:13
Romans 5:17–21	Ephesians 6:13
Romans 6:12–14	James 4:7

PART III

THE CHURCH AT SMYRNA— STUDIES ON ENDURANCE

10

LIFE BEGINS
AFTER SUFFERING

*And to the angel of the church in Smyrna write: The words of
the first and the last, who died and came to life.*

(Revelation 2:8)

Καὶ τῷ ἀγγέλῳ τῆς ἐν Σμύρνῃ ἐκκλησίας γράψον Τάδε
λέγει ὁ πρῶτος καὶ ὁ ἔσχατος, ὃς ἐγένετο νεκρὸς καὶ ἔζη-
σεν.   (ΑΠΟΚΑΛΥΨΙΣ ΙΩΑΝΝΟΥ 2:8)

E ver meet those people who do well under pressure? Are *you* one of
those people? Do you get projects done the night before they're due?
Do you meet your quota three days before you have to report it? I'm not one
of those. Give me a little margin—as much time as possible, please. The
pressure may get *you* all fired up, but it smothers *me*. That's likely why I'm
not a brain surgeon, a lion tamer, or a hostage negotiator. If I were ever on

America's Got Talent,[13] I'd freeze up and forget my name—just like I do at customs when I'm crossing the border. I have no idea how Nik Wallenda can walk a tightrope across the Grand Canyon, how NBA player Stephen Curry can sink game-winning threes, or how singers can belt out the national anthem in front of tens of thousands of fans without a hiccup. There must be a secret to handling the pressure.

In Revelation 2:8, we find a church under pressure—the church at Smyrna. Smyrna was considered to be the most beautiful city in Asia Minor. The ornament of Asia, the crown of Asia, *and* the flower of Asia were its rightful nicknames. A grand city on the Aegean Sea, it possessed the safest harbor in Anatolia and was covered by rolling foothills with temples and buildings on top. Its streets were broad and paved with well-cut stone. It even had an exquisite public library, a stadium, and an Odeon for music and theater. Smyrna was the birthplace of the Greek poet Homer. It was well-known as a learning center for science and medicine, known for its beauty, education, culture, and the arts.

> Myrrh is sap drawn from the Boswellia sacra and Commiphora trees and was used in biblical times for perfume, holy oil, incense, and medicine. It has strong aromatic and remedial properties and is used today to treat a wide variety of conditions, such as ulcers, bad breath, colds, coughs, and even cancer.

The name Smyrna (also *Smyrna* in Greek) means "bitter" because myrrh was its chief export. It also served as a prophetic label for the Christians. Times had become harsh. The Jews living in Smyrna had become hostile toward them because they had been making converts of Jews and those who were interested in Judaism. The Jews wanted to put a stop to this. So, they ganged up with the Romans and a persecution against the Christians began. While the rest of the Smyrnaeans were enjoying the sweet life in Smyrna, the Christians were looking to God to save their lives.

It's ironic that the worst persecution was taking place in the most beautiful city. That seems to encapsulate suffering: when it happens to us, everyone else goes about enjoying their lives. Part of the pain of suffering is having no one else to suffer with. This will either force you to quit or make you look to God for your help. (See Psalm 121:1–2.) The believers in Smyrna looked to Jesus for an answer.

JESUS UNDERSTANDS OUR PAIN

As Jesus begins His message, He tells them it is He *"who died and came to life"* (*hos egeneto nekros kai ezēsen*). This powerful statement may have sent tingles down the Smyrnaeans' legs. There are two verbs here: *egeneto*, which means "became," as in "became dead" (*nekros*), and *ezēsen*, "came to life."

Egeneto places emphasis on the fact that an event happened.[14] Jesus suffered and He died; that's a solid fact. Therefore, the head of the church, who held the Smyrnaeans' fate in His hands, understood their pain and empathized with them. This would be a great relief to them.

Next, we find *ezēsen* functioning in a way that stresses the beginning of an action.[15] It accentuates the moment Christ came back to life in order to emphasize that He got victory after death. You could translate this passage, "became dead, and entered to life," or "became dead, and began to live." There is a principle here: sometimes, things don't live until they've died. And dying is suffering, suffering is pressure, and pressure isn't fun.

It's easy to ignore suffering in the social media age we live in today. Because people pick and choose what they want you to see about their lives, it's easy to think you're the only one suffering. But the truth is, all those who serve Christ will have to endure pressure and pain. While you may never face having to give your life for Christ, you may have to suffer letting a relationship go. It's probable you'll have to take it on the chin when the gang at the office laughs at you for not joining in on their lunchtime shenanigans. Your popularity at school will decline when you refuse to play the drinking games. But the persisting pressure, caused by the death you are dying, is giving birth to something marvelous in your life. New seasons of life aren't only born when the clock strikes midnight on New Year's Eve. They're born after you've suffered a while and done a little dying.

This week, don't despise the time of suffering. Instead of moping around, why not dance, shout, and rejoice that you're never going to be the same again? That's the secret of handling the pressure. (See James 1:2–4.)

When you've come through the suffering, people will wonder if you're the same person they used to know.

PRAYER FOR THE WEEK

Dear Heavenly Father—
I thank You that Jesus has the victory over suffering and death. He is in control of my life and is sovereign over the things I suffer. I declare that my pain won't take me out. It is only working to give me new and better life. Father, may Your grace bring me through this pain and into the victory You have laid up in store for me. In Jesus's name, amen!

ACTIVITY FOR THE WEEK

Dance! God's Word tells us to rejoice when we experience pressure that comes from trials and suffering. (See James 1:2.) Start your day off by dancing before the Lord for at least three minutes. As you rejoice, declare that the Lord is bringing you through!

SCRIPTURES FOR THE WEEK

Psalm 119:28	2 Timothy 2:9–10
2 Corinthians 4:17	1 Peter 1:6–7
2 Thessalonians 3:3	1 Peter 5:10

11

ROBBED, BUT RICH

I know your tribulation *and your* poverty *(but you are* rich)...   (Revelation 2:9a)

Οἶδά σου τὴν θλῖψιν καὶ τὴν πτωχείαν, ἀλλὰ πλούσιος εἶ...   (ΑΠΟΚΑΛΥΨΙΣ ΙΩΑΝΝΟΥ 2:9a)

You're helpless when you're robbed. There's usually no telling who the culprit is; just about anyone could be playing with your stuff. There's no way to find it, no clue where to begin. Even *if* you are miraculously re-united with your stuff, it's been in someone else's hands. You feel violated and the whole thing is creepy. *Why did this ever have to happen,* you wonder.

It's a lot of stress. I know. In the summer of 2009, someone kept punching holes in the window of my SUV. My neighborhood wasn't known for crime. Without thinking, I'd leave my GPS on my windshield when I came home. It felt like someone slugged me in the guts when I walked outside one morning and saw my dashboard swimming in shattered glass. The

GPS was gone; my CDs and my favorite sunglasses were gone, too. I took it personally. I felt responsible. For weeks, I wondered what I did to deserve being robbed.

Then, it happened again.

I rolled out of bed and looked for my new iPhone 3. I had come in late the night before…and it dawned on me that I had left it on the seat of my SUV. A scorching, anxious rush dried up my mouth faster than if I had opened it under an airport hand dryer. I dashed outside in hopes I could be wrong. The emerald pool of glistening glass stopped me at its shores. I became unnerved. Thoughts bombarded me like tweets from an angry troll. *This is your fault. Someone is watching you. What are you going to tell the windshield repair person this time? You've now lost over $1,000 in stuff. You could have spent that on a vacation.*

In Revelation 2:8, people were stealing from the believers in Smyrna. It wasn't easy being a Christian there. Christianity was considered a cult that had spun out of Judaism. Society was against them and their homes were the targets of raids. Mobs plundered their belongings and destroyed their property. This was normal life for a first-century Christian. (See Hebrews 10:34.) Imagine a raid of angry unbelievers kicking in your door from time to time because you go to church every Sunday and take communion. They've carried away your flat screen so many times you don't even know if you should buy another.

The emotional and psychological pressure had taken its toll on the Smyrnaeans. This is indicated by the Greek word for "tribulation" (*thlipsis*). This meant to be under a crushing weight. It's the feeling of a thousand cinder blocks stacked in a tower on your soul. It was used to describe the troubling pain of war and childbirth. It even described the intensity that political candidates felt when rival parties launched their smear campaigns.

In medicine, "oncothlipsis" (*oncos* meaning "mass" and *thlipsis* meaning "pressure") is compression and tightening created by the presence of a tumor. Often, oncothlipsis causes severe pain and discomfort.

Following *thlipsis*, we find the conjunction "and" (*kai*). Small as it seems, it's significant. This explains and amplifies *why* the Smyrnaeans were feeling the pressure of the concrete blocks. It was because of their "poverty" (*ptōcheia*). There are two Greek words for poverty. First, is *penēs*. This means to be poor in the sense of having nothing above what is necessary. It would describe someone who lives paycheck to paycheck and doesn't ever buy new clothes. Life could be worse, right? This worse living is described by *ptōcheia*. This means to have absolutely nothing at all. It described birds that didn't have their own nest. The believers in Smyrna had been ransacked so many times, they didn't have a home, a nanny goat, or a jar of oil.

JESUS: LOOK ON THE BRIGHT SIDE

Yet, Jesus says something that would have probably shocked them. He begins by using a conjunction, "*but*" (*alla*). This is used to make a sharp contrast. It comes off strong. It's like Jesus was saying, "Look on the bright side!" He wanted to cheer them up with a stunning revelation. Then He calls them "rich (*plousios*)—abounding with more than what the normal person has. Every time Satan raided them, Jesus multiplied it back. Reimbursement wasn't always the material things they lost; their virtues and eternal rewards always grew richer.

The Lord wants you to look on the bright side of things: He can give faster than Satan can steal. When we remain faithful to Him, despite the assaults of life, He lays up eternal treasures in heaven for us. Jesus said one of the secrets to a meaningful life is to attach our joy to eternal things and godliness instead of material things that could end up being stolen. (See Matthew 6:19–20.) Have you ever seen someone whose boat is going over the falls, yet they keep smiling from ear to ear? Ever seen someone play a bad hand with contentment in their countenance? Their joy is in the right things.

This week, don't let the things Satan has stolen from you burden you down. Look on the bright side. Jesus has given you more reasons to rejoice than the devil has given you reasons to be sad. Every day, you are getting richer—your godliness is growing and your heavenly account is on the up and up.

PRAYER FOR THE WEEK

Dear Heavenly Father—
You have made me rich! I'll say it again: You have made me rich! I declare that the enemy hasn't stolen anything that You haven't already replaced many times over. You are a faithful and loving God and You always have my back. I won't consider what the enemy has taken. This week, I'll only count Your blessings. And because of this, great will be Your peace and joy in my life. In Jesus's name, amen!

ACTIVITY FOR THE WEEK

Void a check. Make it out to yourself and make it from "Jesus Christ, who died and came to life." In the amount section, write, "Everything that was stolen." Put the check in a place where you can see it every day. Every time you look at it, thank the Lord He has made you rich.

SCRIPTURES FOR THE WEEK

1 Samuel 2:8	2 Corinthians 6:4–10
Isaiah 14:32	2 Corinthians 8:9
Matthew 5:3	James 2:5

12

HOW TO HANDLE YOUR ASSASSINS

[I know]... the slander of those who say that they are Jews and are not, but are a synagogue of Satan. (Revelation 2:9b)

[Οἶδά]... καὶ τὴν βλασφημίαν ἐκ τῶν λεγόντων Ἰουδαίους εἶναι ἑαυτοὺς καὶ οὐκ εἰσὶν ἀλλὰ συναγωγὴ τοῦ Σατανᾶ. (ΑΠΟΚΑΛΥΨΙΣ ΙΩΑΝΝΟΥ 2:9b)

There are assassins out there. They don't drive James Bond's car or throw ninja stars, but their words are lethal darts. They're dangerous hitmen. They put our character in the crosshairs, hoping for a vital shot that drops our reputation into the dirt. They've made a place for our heads on the wall of shame.

Do you know who I'm talking about? Slanderers. Scorners. Gossips. People who mock.

You're not exempt from the firing squad just because you're godly. Godliness is what puts you within range. God's Word promises that if we serve Him, we're going to encounter those who talk about us like we're a bad smell. (See 2 Timothy 3:12.) I'm not sure about that old saying, "Sticks and stones may break my bones, but..." Names *do* hurt. They hurt worse. I've been hit in the head with a rock a time or two (I hope it's not obvious). I'd much prefer the stone using my head to change direction than having to relive the times a group of scoffers used my name for target practice. Being talked about is humiliating. It's like wearing a white T-shirt with a spaghetti stain on it.

In addition to having their possessions ransacked, the believers in Smyrna were being slandered. The Greek word for "slander" is *blasphēmia*. It's where we get our word "blasphemy." It means cruel speech. Today, we'd call it verbal abuse and bullying. It's the strongest word possible to describe character assassination. It's disrespectful, total disregard for someone's reputation. Comments of this sort are flagged on social media platforms today.

> "Blaspheme-vine" is a greenbrier plant that grows in damp regions of the USA. It's savagely armed with quills and thorns and is so nicknamed because those who get caught in it often spout off impolite words.

The assassins were pious Jews who hated Christianity. They were jealous. The Christians were growing in numbers and taking their converts away. The Jews reacted by puffing themselves up and putting the Christians down. They did everything to tarnish the Smyrnaean Christians. They alleged that Christians were cannibals for taking communion. They claimed that their communal meal, known as a "love feast," was nothing but a big orgy. And they indicted the Christians for being rebellious to Rome because they would call only Jesus "Lord."

The pious Jews felt they had a right to slander the Christians. This is indicated by the phrase *"those who say that they are Jews."* By saying *they* are the Jews, they are saying *they* are the descendants of Abraham and the people of God. Therefore, *they* have the right to slander the Christians. Mockers always think they are better than those they are putting down. The people shooting holes in your reputation think they have a good reason to do so. In their minds, God likes them more than He likes you.

JESUS PUTS SLANDERERS IN THEIR PLACE

Jesus weighs in on this. In reference to the Jews' claim, He says they *"are not" (eisin ouk).*[16] Jesus was saying, "No, this isn't true. You are *not* My people. You are *not* better than the Christians." He was setting the record straight. Jesus will put your slanderers in their place. Remember, He *knows* us. He has walked intimately among us. When you are suffering someone's malicious gossip, let Jesus weigh in.

Then, Jesus takes it further. He tells the self-righteous Jews that they are actually part of the synagogue of Satan. When we hear the word "synagogue," we think of a Jewish place of worship. In the first century, "synagogue" meant a gathering of people, an assembly, or a group. Jesus was telling the mockers that they were part of Satan's mob. People who aim to destroy other people's reputation, even if it is for a "holier than thou" reason, are serving the devil. It makes sense: the name "devil" (*diabolos*) means slanderer and accuser. People join his crew when they do the same.

If there is an assassin taking shots at you today, it's important to remember who is who. Assassins serve the devil. Ultimately, it's Satan taking aim at you. Don't get provoked and try to take action. You'll make matters worse. Be like the Smyrnaeans and let Jesus weigh in. In the Lord's time, He will set the record straight. Just keep on smiling because Jesus knows the truth. And until He brings the truth to light, pray for your enemies and be good to them. (See Matthew 5:44.) That's what you do when you are playing for team Jesus.

PRAYER FOR THE WEEK

Dear Heavenly Father—
I have assassins. People are taking shots at my character. I know it is the enemy at work through them. I thank You that You see all things

and know the truth. This week, I will pray for those who are spreading lies about me. May You touch their lives and their families' lives, and show them mercy and grace. I place my reputation in Your hands and declare that You will preserve who I am. In Jesus's name, amen!

ACTIVITY FOR THE WEEK

Make a list of the people taking shots at you. What are they saying? Cancel every word they have spoken over your life by declaring it is under the blood of Jesus. Next, ask God to show you His heart for your slanderers. Commit to praying for them every day this week.

SCRIPTURES FOR THE WEEK

Leviticus 19:18

Jeremiah 51:36

Proverbs 20:22

Romans 12:17–19

2 Timothy 4:14

Hebrews 10:30

13

DO YOU MAGNIFY THE CAPTAIN OR THE WAVES?

Do not fear what you are about to suffer. (Revelation 2:10a)

μηδὲν φοβοῦ ἃ μέλλεις πάσχειν.
(ΑΠΟΚΑΛΥΨΙΣ ΙΩΑΝΝΟΥ 2:10a)

Most of us know a wet blanket—that one person who dwells on the worst possible outcomes and feeds on hearty platefuls of negativity. While you stand in awe at the season's first snowfall—marveling at flakes tumbling from the sky like winter paratroopers—they are worried that their car might hit ice and end up front end first under a truck. On the first day of vacation, while your toes are squishing and flicking the warm, velvet sand, they're talking about what it's going to feel like getting back to work.

God forbid they ever have an ache: they'll be on WebMD, swearing they've only three months to live.

Pessimists believe pessimism is what keeps them from buying a ticket into fantasyland. They'd rather live in fear than pretend life is rivers of chocolate and candy-coated trees. But pessimism is *also* fantasyland—just streams of sewage and fruit that tastes like roadkill. Pessimists, how many of your fearful fantasies have *actually* happened?

We weren't created to dwell on suffering or highlight misfortune. Fabricating worst-case scenarios will steal our peace and there is no end to it. Either our focus is on misery and misfortune, or it's on God's Word. But it shouldn't be both—and it *can't* be both. Our eyes should be on Jesus. There's no excuse for pessimism.

Despite the Smyrnaeans' trials, Jesus expected them to maintain the right attitude. It might sound a bit unrealistic. They've been ransacked, they're impoverished, and the city is slandering them—not very encouraging conditions. But Christ's expectations are a testament to the greatness of His power and the strength of His might.

In Revelation 2:10, Jesus says, *"Do not fear"* (*mēden phobou*). This is a strong command to stop doing something. The word "fear" (*phobos*) is in the present tense, telling us that the action Jesus forbids was already going on; they were full of fear and were expecting even worse things to happen. It's easy to imagine they were losing sleep, participating in abysmal conversations, and diminishing God's ability in their lives.

Jesus wanted this to stop. He uses a strong negative to tell them that they were "not" (*meden*) to fear.[17] This is an emphatic. Jesus is saying, "Do *not* fear!" "*Stop* fearing once and for all!" "*Stop* all fear right now!" The Lord has no tolerance for fear; it reduces His ability in our lives. He is a faithful God. He expects us to trust in Him, even when our life is on the line. Pessimism is never appropriate. In difficult times, we must allow His voice into our lives to show us what to do, instead of preparing for our doom.

HAVE NO FEAR...IT'S GOING TO GET WORSE

After such a strong command not to fear, you might expect Jesus to say things are going to get better. Nope. Jesus tells them they're about to get a whole lot worse. He tells the believers in Smyrna that they are *"about to suffer"* (*melleis paschein*) even more. The Greek word "about" (*melleis*) means inevitability and suggests something is inescapable. The Greek word "suffer" (*paschein*) means "to experience a blow to fate." Inevitable suffering was whooshing toward the Smyrnaean church. An inescapable storm had closed in and there was no way around it. Imprisonment was stirring the sea. Waves of death were starting to swell. The Smyrnaeans were headed right for the eye. Yet, Jesus wanted them to expect the best. They weren't to think about throwing themselves overboard. It was inappropriate for them talk about the force of the wind and the sway of the current. They were to marvel at the ability of their captain. There was treasure beyond the storm. And the Lord was leading them to it.

> In Greek mythology, Phobos was the god of fear and his brother, Deimos, was the god of panic. They were the sons of Ares, the god of war. Together, Phobos and Deimos would accompany Ares into battle to spread fear and panic. Ancient Greek heroes and warriors fought with Phobos on their shields to incite terror. Phobos's followers believed that he took pleasure in blood. This gives us a picture behind the tormenting nature of fear.

Difficulty is inevitable. There are things that enter our lives that we have no more control over than the weather. When those things blow in, you have a choice: will you magnify the contrary conditions, or will you magnify the Lord? It's not a choice of being an optimist rather than a pessimist. It's a choice to put your faith in Christ and trust in His might. All of us have a testimony. Will yours be about the strength of the waves, or the ability of the Captain?

PRAYER FOR THE WEEK

Dear Heavenly Father
I thank You that You have called me to put my trust in You. You are a God who finds delight in my faith, as Your Word says in Hebrews 11:6. In this moment, I make the choice to stop all fear. I renounce every negative word that I have spoken regarding my circumstances. I will

*fill my lips with words of praise. From this point forward, I'll magnify
You and not my challenges. In Jesus's name, amen!*

ACTIVITY FOR THE WEEK

Make a praise list. Write down twenty specific things for which God
is to be magnified for having done for you in the past. (For example: 1.
Healing me from asthma; 2. Saving my grandma; 3. Helping me get a
promotion at work.) When you are finished, add blanks for twenty more
things. Expect God to amaze you *this* week with twenty more brand new
things to give Him praise for.

SCRIPTURES FOR THE WEEK

Exodus 14:13   Isaiah 41:10

Deuteronomy 1:21   Matthew 14:27

Joshua 1:9   Luke 12:32

14

WHO'S TO BLAME FOR EVIL?

Behold, the devil is about to throw some of you into prison, that you may be tested... (Revelation 2:10b)

ἰδοὺ μέλλει βάλλειν ὁ διάβολος ἐξ ὑμῶν εἰς φυλακὴν ἵνα πειρασθῆτε... (ΑΠΟΚΑΛΥΨΙΣ ΙΩΑΝΝΟΥ 2:10b)

Why *is God doing this to me?* Human beings love to begin questions with *why*, especially when they pertain to tragedy and disaster. And God is usually part of the conversation. He's the drip pan: He catches all the fault and blame when there's nowhere else for it to go.

I've seen many horrific events in the news. Few have been as shocking as the Sandy Hook Elementary school shooting on December 14, 2012. I cried when I heard the news.

That evening, I was going to the Chicago Symphony and Orchestra with some friends, one of whom was an atheist. "Where was God today?" she asked. She was indicting God for not stopping the evil. I told her she didn't really want God to stop evil. Based on our conversations, she was content fornicating and cheating on her taxes. If God decided to stop *evil*, he'd stop *all evil*—and she wouldn't be happy.

God's Word doesn't treat Him like the drip pan, letting blame fall on Him whenever tragic things happen. God *is* going to deal with evil once and for all. (See Revelation 20:10.) *When* He does, He will have to judge with severity those left in sin. (See Matthew 25:46.) So, God puts up with evil so people have a chance to repent and be saved. Until the time of judgment comes, God will be patient and forbearing. (See 2 Peter 3:9.) Meanwhile, Satan will continue to stir up evil to make the world hateful toward Christ.

Revelation 2:10 makes it clear that *Satan* is the troublemaker. He is the one causing suffering, not God. The Lord tells the Smyrnaeans that *the devil* is the one who is going to throw them into prison. This is noted by, *"Behold, the devil" (idou ho diabolos). Idou* functions sort of like an emotional outburst; it aims emphasis at the words that follow. In this case, "the devil." It's as if God got His cell phone out, scrolled through His photos, pulled up the devil's picture, and said, "See? *This* is the guy who's causing your problems! He's the author of your trouble!"

Next, Jesus tells the Smyrnaeans that the devil is about to throw *"some of you"* into prison. "Some of" is the Greek word *ek* and means "out of." It implies "some" which have come "out of" a whole. This means that "some" of the Smyrnaeans would be taken from out of the rest of the church and thrown into prison.

Satan doesn't have to aim at everyone. A direct hit on one will send shockwaves to all. Think about it: a family of ten agonizes when one child is on drugs. A church is jolted when its pastor has an affair. A country mourns when one school is victimized by a mass shooting. Satan knows that people react to his horror, often by turning away from God.

DEVIL TRIES TO DESTROY US

This is what Jesus tells the Smyrnaeans. The devil is about to throw some of you in prison *"that you may be tested."* "That" (*hina*) is a very important word expressing an intended purpose; it shows the devil's intent. Throwing believers into prison had a bigger meaning: the devil wanted to test the Smyrnaeans. "Test" (*peirazo*) doesn't mean to put someone through a challenge so they can win your approval. It means to tempt someone in order to destroy them, to change someone's mind about something. The devil was locking up the Christians in Smyrna so that the whole community would change their mind about God. This could only be the work of the devil, the accuser.

> Smyrna was the place of one of the most well-known martyrdoms in church history. The martyrdom befell Polycarp, a pupil of John and Greek bishop of the church in Smyrna, during the second century. At first, the proconsul sought to burn Polycarp alive. When, miraculously, the fires failed to afflict him, the executioner stuck him with a dagger.

How would you react if you lived in first-century Smyrna and some of the people you went to church with were hauled off to prison to be killed? Would you think God is unfair? Would you wonder if it was still worthwhile to keep serving Christ? It's possible some of the Smyrnaeans might have thought this. And if they did, the devil's accusations against Christ would be working. He'd have them right where he wanted.

When you see tragedy, remember *who's* behind it and remember *why* they are behind it. If a family member stumbles, don't become bitter at God. If your pastor sins, don't toss everything he has taught you to the wind. If there happens to be more terror in your nation, pray it doesn't turn your nation's heart from the Lord. Satan stirs up evil, victimizes people, and then accuses God a thousand different ways just to get you to walk away from serving the Lord. No matter what happens this week, remember that God is the solution, not the problem. The devil is the problem.

PRAYER FOR THE WEEK

Dear Heavenly Father—
I thank You that You are good and the source of all that is good, as Your Word says in James 1:17. I refuse to believe that You are the cause of my trouble and pain. I realize that Satan is the adversary and the one who wages war against humanity. Today, I pray You give me revelation to see You at work amidst all the wickedness in this world. From here on out, I will declare that You are good and Your mercy endures forever, as it is written in Psalm 100:5. Nothing that the enemy attempts will change my confession. In Jesus's name, Amen.

ACTIVITY FOR THE WEEK

Think of five tragic events that have taken place in the last six months. You may use those in your own life and those in current events. Make a list of people involved. Pray for them. Ask God to open their eyes to see His goodness, despite the work of the devil.

SCRIPTURES FOR THE WEEK

Genesis 3:1–7

John 10:10

Job 1:6–12

1 John 3:8

Acts 10:28

Revelation 12:9

15

IT ONLY LASTS TEN DAYS

...and for ten days *you will have tribulation.*

(Revelation 2:10c)

...καὶ ἕξετε θλῖψιν ἡμερῶν δέκα *γίνου.*

(ΑΠΟΚΑΛΥΨΙΣ ΙΩΑΝΝΟΥ 2:10c)

I love hot showers. My water bill is probably higher than yours. I usually average twenty-five minutes—even longer when it's freezing outside. If only I could figure out how to move my couch into the shower, then I wouldn't need the other rooms in my house.

My tenure in shower-taking has given me an expertise in steam. I know all kinds of neat ways to take advantage of vapor. I can use it to write Bible verses in Greek on the mirror, or I can use it to fluff out the wrinkles in my suit. I can even put drops of eucalyptus in the tub and clear out my nasal passages. But you don't have to be an expert steamologist to know that steam lasts only a moment before it embraces the door and collapses back into the clouds.

The seasons of life vanish like vapor. (See James 4:14.) Your toddlers are now talking; where did they learn to say things like that? Your commencement is now coming; weren't you just deciding where to study? Another wedding, another anniversary, one more funeral. Vapor has found the door and isn't taking its time to go back into the sky. Everything happens so fast. If there's one thing God's Word emphasizes, it's that this life is soberingly short.

Even shorter are the *seasons* of life. In Revelation 2:10c, Jesus reminds the Smyrnaeans about this in order to encourage them. They were in a season of acute persecution and wondering when it would pass. Jesus tells them that their tribulation will last "ten days." This is significant. It tells us the time the Smyrnaeans were going to have to endure tribulation was limited to "days," (*hēmerōn*)—not weeks, months, or years.[18] If you think about it in light of the totality of life, "days" is a pretty short measure of time. Have you ever wasted a few days doing nothing? Plenty of people stay in their pajamas from Christmas until New Year's. It's only a week, right? Jesus was reminding the Smyrnaeans that, although seasons of suffering feel long because they are difficult, they are short.

> Hemeralopia (*hēmera* meaning "day," *alalos* meaning "blind," and *ōps* meaning "eye") is the inability to see well in bright light. It is often caused by cataracts.

DANIEL WAS TESTED FOR 10 DAYS, TOO

Seasons of suffering aren't just short; they're also significant. Jesus alludes to this by using the number "ten" (*deka*). This is a reference to Daniel 1:12–15. Here, Daniel and his three friends refused to eat food from the king's table because it was considered an act of worship of the king. They desired to remain faithful to Jehovah. So, Daniel told his superior to test him and his friends for ten days. He had a plan: while everyone else ate from the king's table, they would eat only vegetables and drink water. At the end of the ten days, the supervisor could compare them to those who ate the king's food and see who was in better shape. Daniel's superior agreed. At the end of ten days, Daniel's superior found Daniel and his friends to be much healthier and looking better than everyone else.

This mirrored the situation in Smyrna. The Smyrnaean believers refused to worship Caesar or participate in any activity that hailed him as Lord. They'd rather face the consequences of Rome than compromise and let Jesus down. Jesus took notice. He reminded them of Daniel's ten days of testing to let them know that, after the brief period of refusing to compromise was over, they were going to come out on top. They wouldn't be overcome. In fact, they would fare better than everyone who was conforming to Caesar. Their brief moment of suffering would produce results that last. And that's what Jesus was after. The only thing that stood between them and their results was a short period of time.

You may be facing some pain that seems like it's been going on for quite some time—it's just not your season. Did the love of your life walk away from you because you wouldn't have sex outside of marriage? Is your boss at work treating you unfairly because they see the light of Christ in your eyes? Maybe your checking account has gotten used to being overdrafted because you stepped out in faith to start your ministry. Remember, it's just a vapor. It's only ten days. The pain you're feeling won't last forever, but it will produce results that do last. You'll get through these days and you'll have years to tell everyone about it. Don't give up…the suffering won't last long.

PRAYER FOR THE WEEK

Dear Heavenly Father—
I thank You that though sorrow lasts for a brief night, joy comes in the morning, as You tell us in Psalm 30:5. Though I have suffering at the moment, it is only for a moment. I am passing through it, and I will not compromise or complain. I ask You for Your continued strength to help me to remain faithful to You until these ten days are over. And when they are, I'll be closer to You and fit with everything I need to succeed. In Jesus's name, amen!

ACTIVITY FOR THE WEEK

Reflect on and journal about one of the most difficult seasons in your life. What did you go through? Was it one event or a series of events? How long did it last? Does it seem as long now as it did then? How did God's grace work in your life during that time? What fruitful things did it produce in you that you wouldn't have if you hadn't gone through it?

SCRIPTURES FOR THE WEEK

Psalm 30:5	Ecclesiastes 3:1–8
Psalm 126:5	2 Corinthians 4:17
Hosea 6:2	1 Peter 5:10

16

JUST KEEP ON GOING

Be faithful unto death, and I will give you the crown of life.
(Revelation 2:10d)

γίνου πιστὸς ἄχρι θανάτου, καὶ δώσω σοι τὸν στέφανον τῆς ζωῆς.   (ΑΠΟΚΑΛΥΨΙΣ ΙΩΑΝΝΟΥ 2:10d)

Do you have the Nike+ Run Club app? It's my favorite app that I never use. There are so many interactive little features on it that make me wish I could muster up enough willpower to become a runner. For example, you can program each pair of your shoes and keep track of how many miles you've put on them. You can challenge your friends to a race, compete with them on a regular basis, and win colorful awards. And if you need some help, you can download a virtual coach who will push you to become the next Usain Bolt.

Before I became such a loaf, I once gave it a try. I even went to the Nike outlet and invested some hard-earned cash on a $40 pair of fluorescent yellow shoes…to match nothing I wear.

My first run was on the evening of June 27, 2014. I ran 3.30 miles in Miami, Florida. Not too bad for a first run, right? My next run came the following morning: 3.64 miles. This was followed by a two-mile run two days later. When I looked at my friends' stats, I noticed I was going to need to do a lot more running to take the lead. So, I did the unthinkable: I laced up my shoes and pushed myself to the point of death. I made a choice to keep going until my legs gave out. I fought cramps, tightness in my chest, and the beating heat of the sun. My distress didn't matter—I wanted to win. So, I just kept running.

When I crawled into the house after my kamikaze adventure, my shirt was drenched, my face was pale, and I was nearly throwing up. It was also the beginning of a bad case of runner's knee, which sent me into early retirement two weeks later. But that doesn't change the facts: for one whole week, Chris Palmer was the champion runner among his eight friends on the Nike+ Run Club App, all because he decided to look death squarely in the eye and run over the top of it in his fluorescent yellow shoes.

AN URGENT COMMAND FOR FAITH

In Revelation 2:10d, Jesus talks to the Smyrnaeans about the distance he expects their faithfulness to go. He says, *"Be faithful unto death."* The Greek words "be faithful" (*ginou pistos*) express an urgent command for continual action.[19] It's like saying, "Be faithful! Be faithful! And keep being faithful, faithful, faithful!"

Think of a runner who sets out on a sprint with no intention to stop, like Forrest Gump.[20] First, Forrest ran to the end of the road, then he ran to the town limits, and then to the end of Greenbow County. Since he had run that far, Forrest tells the lady sitting beside him on the bench, "I ran clear across Alabama…I just kept on goin'." Next, Forrest runs to the Pacific Ocean. "And when I got there, I figured since I gone this far, might as well turn around, jus' keep on goin'." Then Forrest runs to the Atlantic Ocean. "When I got to another ocean, I figured since I'd gone this far, I might as well just turn back, keep right on goin'."

The elderly woman next to him laughs and says, "So, you just—ran!"

"Yea!" Forrest says.

Jesus wants our faithfulness toward Him to "keep right on goin'" without any regard for duration or time.

Jesus intensifies the extent of faithfulness when He tells the Smyrnaeans that they are to be faithful *"unto death"* (*achri thanatou*). *Achri* means "as far as." It emphasizes *the conditions* the Smyrnaeans needed to remain faithful in—when facing death. The whole idea is, "be faithful, faithful, faithful, even when the conditions around you are deadly." It's like my seven-mile run: I was willing to keep going even while my lungs were imploding and my legs were collapsing. Jesus wants our faithfulness to keep on goin' over the top of the worst conditions the enemy sends our way.

> The crown given to Olympic victors in ancient Greece was called a *kotinos*. It was made up of olive branches from trees near Mt. Olympus. Olive oil from these trees was a symbol of prosperity and glory. Therefore, a *kotinos* was the most illustrious prize a Greek citizen could receive.

The Lord promises the *"crown of life"* (*ton stephanon tēs zōēs*) to those who don't throw in the towel. "Life," or *tes zoes*, explains what the crown is: eternal life.[21] The reason eternal life is compared to a crown is because crowns were placed on the heads of the runners who were victorious in the Olympic Games. These runners pushed their bodies to the point of death to attain the prize. And when the crown was laid upon them, it came with joy and delight. If we want the joy and delight of eternal life, we must have the resilience of a champion.

What are some of the unfavorable conditions that have obstructed your way or foiled your faith? Have they turned your sprint into a power walk, or maybe a stumble? Don't stop now. There is a crown of life ahead and it has your name on it. This week is a perfect time to pick up the pace. It doesn't matter what the conditions are; the Holy Spirit wants to give you the strength to keep on going and tread on death. (See Luke 10:19.)

PRAYER FOR THE WEEK

Dear Heavenly Father—
Your Holy Spirit has given me the means and ability to be faithful to
You. No matter what situations I face today, my faithfulness won't be
stopped—I'll remain committed to You. My greatest joy is the hope
that eternal life brings. Thank You that You have made it possible to
live with You, forever. In Jesus's name, amen!

ACTIVITY FOR THE WEEK

Go for a run or a walk. As you're out, pay attention to the different obstacles you must endure (rain, dirt roads, cars, cramps, etc.). When you are
at the point of giving up, push yourself one more time. How does this relate
to your spiritual life? What are some of the obstacles of life that test your
faithfulness? Where can you get the strength to help your faith keep going?

SCRIPTURES FOR THE WEEK

Matthew 25:21	Galatians 5:7
Acts 20:24	1 Timothy 6:12
1 Corinthians 9:24–26	2 Timothy 4:7–8

17

UNHAPPY ENDINGS ARE COMING TO AN END

The one who conquers will not be hurt by the second death.
(Revelation 2:11b)

ὁ νικῶν οὐ μὴ ἀδικηθῇ ἐκ τοῦ θανάτου τοῦ δευτέρου.
(ΑΠΟΚΑΛΥΨΙΣ ΙΩΑΝΝΟΥ 2:11b)

And they all lived *happily ever after*. It's the most popular way to end a story. Mario saves the princess, Belle tells the Beast she loves him before the last petal falls, and Jake Sully winds up with Neytiri. When our minds are innocent, we grow up expecting that it's all going to end the way it should, the way we want. And so, we fall asleep and dream of how it will end for us—happily, of course.

Then something happens: you wake up and begin to walk through life. Your first heartbreak. The rejection letter from your college of choice. The close friend who's killed in a car wreck. Dad and mom call it quits. Tsunamis wipe out civilizations along the coast. Terrorism…politicians who cheat…nuclear stand-offs…genocide…starvation around the world.… Life becomes more like a Billy Joel song than a Disney cartoon.

My homiletics professor must have known his young class of hopeful preachers were starting to realize this. Every day—and I mean every single day—Dr. David Watson walked from the back of the room into the front of the class, bellowing out his famous phrase: "*Life* is *not* fair—but God! Is! Faithful!" We used to imitate him in our dorms and tease him behind his back but, as time has progressed, I've come to hang on to those words with a stronger grip. I have to; I've seen too many good Christians face unhappy endings, like the health-and-wealth preacher who dies in a plane crash, the Coptic Christians blown up by bomb blasts, and the praying grandmother who loses a battle to heart failure.

> There are over fifty ways to say "no" in the English language. Can you think of at least twenty-five?

God's Word is not a fairy tale and its endings aren't always happy. In fact, the earliest death in the Bible was tragic: the God-fearing Abel was unjustly murdered by his jealous brother, Cain. (See Genesis 4:8.) Abel's death sets a precedent throughout Scripture that unfair things happen to those who serve God. We see that taking place as the rest of Scripture unfolds. For example, the righteous king, Josiah, who called for national repentance in Israel, was killed by archers. (See 2 Chronicles 35:24.) And one of the most popular preachers, John the Baptist, had his head lopped off. (See Matthew 14:10.)

ESCAPING THE FIRES OF HELL

The Smyrnaeans were no different; some of them were headed to prison to die a painful death. It's conceivable that they were identifying with King Josiah, Abel, or John the Baptist. But most of all, they probably were identifying with Jesus. And Jesus gives them a message that provides them with encouragement beyond their torment: *"The one who conquers will not be hurt by the second death."* The "second death" refers to torment and pain that comes after the first death (physical death). It is the eternal damnation in the lake of fire and separation from the presence of God. It is everlasting punishment for those who persist in living wickedly. (See Revelation 21:8.) Its chastisements are far beyond any suffering we've come to know in this life and it's a reality that every human being will face, which is why we must choose Christ. The Smyrnaeans had chosen Christ and, for this, Christ assures them that "they will not (*ou mē*) be hurt" by it.

"Not" (*ou mē*) is a combination of two negatives: *ou* and *mē*. When *ou* is used on its own, it denies an alleged reality; when *mē* used on its own, it denies an alleged thought. When you place them together, it denies a reality and a thought. So, in the Smyrnaeans' case, it denies that they will suffer the realities of hell and it refutes any fearful thought they might have otherwise. In other words, Jesus was saying, "Those who overcome will *not* be hurt by hell. So, don't worry over the thought it." Jesus was preparing their eternity and it wouldn't look like their current abysmal situation. They would not be met by the injustices of the current life, they'd have no persecution, and they would be safe from any kind of harm.

Eternity is fair and God is going to make sure that everyone receives the retribution they deserve. Remember, nothing truly ends until we stand before Christ.

Unhappy endings will come to an end when the Judge makes everything right. Until then, keep your confidence in God. If you've been treated unfairly for the color of your skin, rejoice that *God* will honor you. If your close friend has died in a tragic accident, take comfort that God *is* compensating them with more life than they could ever lose. If you were born in poverty, Christ *will* make you rich. You must realize, God is writing your story; and its ending will far outshine the endings you see in the movies. If not in this life, most definitely in the next.

PRAYER FOR THE WEEK

Dear Heavenly Father—
My story is in Your hands. You are the author of my life and You have written a beautiful end for me. I thank You that, when it's all said and

done, I will rule and reign with You in eternity, and all the injustice and suffering will be past. This week, I declare my confidence is in You and that all things are working together for my good. In Jesus's name, amen!

ACTIVITY FOR THE WEEK

Rewrite a story. Pick an event in your life that you have perceived, up to this point, as having a tragic ending. Rewrite the ending in light of the fact that eternity has the final say. Make sure to include what it will be like when you stand before Christ and He makes it right.

SCRIPTURES FOR THE WEEK

Isaiah 25:8

Isaiah 60:20

Jeremiah 31:12

Romans 8:28

2 Corinthians 2:14

Revelation 21:4

PART IV

THE CHURCH AT PERGAMUM—STUDIES ON WORLDVIEW

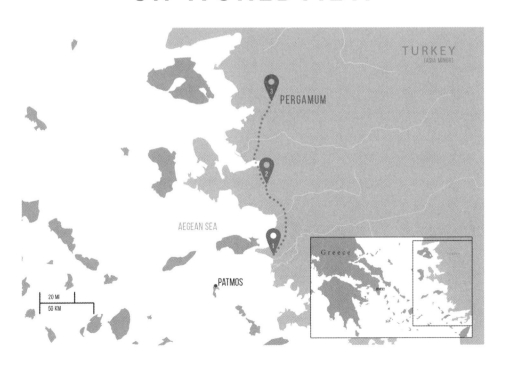

18

JESUS HAS THE LAST TWEET

And to the angel of the church in Pergamum write: The words of him who has the sharp two-edged sword. (Revelation 2:12)

Καὶ τῷ ἀγγέλῳ τῆς ἐν Περγάμῳ ἐκκλησίας γράψον Τάδε λέγει ὁ ἔχων τὴν ῥομφαίαν τὴν δίστομον τὴν ὀξεῖαν.
(ΑΠΟΚΑΛΥΨΙΣ ΙΩΑΝΝΟΥ 2:12)

Need some attention on social media? No problem. Just take a clear stance on some hot, breaking news and your notifications will light up like nighttime on the Las Vegas strip. Nothing will stir up your followers like a controversial post. Threads can rack up hundreds, thousands, and even tens of thousands of comments in a matter of a few hours. Everyone has something to say about everything because everyone has a worldview.

A worldview is the way we perceive life. It's our perspective, made up of our religious beliefs, philosophical ideals, political stances, and sacred values. It determines who we are and how we behave. Everyone *has* a worldview, though some are much louder about it than others.

While Facebook has become many things, it certainly is a battlefield where rival worldviews clash. The wars rage on for hours, days, weeks, and months. It's almost certain to end in casualties of blocked users. I've still not met anyone who's ever changed their mind because of a Facebook fight. If they're out there, their numbers are few. But I understand it. There's right and wrong in this world and people want to defend the truth. So, who gets the final tweet? In Revelation 2:12, we are given a clue.

Here, we find the church in Pergamum. If the Smyrnaeans thought they had it tough, they could have gone to Pergamum and discovered worse. Pergamum was the center for Caesar-worship, the first city in Asia Minor to build a temple to worship the Roman ruler. No place in all of Asia had more passionate worship for Caesar and no place had stricter penalties for those who refused.

There were other forms of worship going on as well. Perhaps the most popular form of worship was to Asclepios, the god of healing. People came in droves to Pergamum to seek Asclepios' healing powers. His followers called him "savior," making Christians cringe. Pergamum also had an altar to Zeus where sacrifices burned all day. It was four stories high and sat on Pergamum's cone-shaped hill, eight hundred feet above the city.

The philosophical temperature in Pergamum was just as hot. It had *the* grandest library in all of Asia. In fact, it was the second greatest library in the whole world, second only to the one in Alexandria. At one point, it held over 200,000 parchment rolls full of knowledge from every field.

> It is said that Marc Antony gave the 200,000 volumes of Pergamum to his wife Cleopatra as a gift in 43 B.C. These volumes were then placed in the Library of Alexandria. It's assumed that most of these volumes were destroyed when the library burned to the ground. Think of what was lost!

Pergamum's variety of worship and the breadth of philosophy made it a center of culture and an arena for worldviews to meet. Christians didn't have an easy time in this arena. They were unpopular for their righteous stances. It's no different today; Christians are frowned upon and despised in places where there is a mix of worldviews.

Consider modern universities. Christians have flunked classes or faced higher consequences for taking the creationist position or trying to protect the rights of the unborn. And don't expect a Christian to teach science or philosophy in a public university. Those schools work hard to keep them out.

JESUS HAS THE FINAL WORD

Despite society's contempt for the Christian's worldview, Jesus reassures the believers in Pergamum. He begins by using a phrase that He begins all of His messages to the seven churches with: *"The words"* (*tade legei*). Beginning like this intensifies the seriousness of the message that is to come. Jesus is telling the believers that there is something crucial they need to realize in light of the situation in Pergamum. And it is that *Jesus* has the sharp, two-edged sword!

The Greek word for "sword" is *rhomphaia*. This refers to a large broad sword that was perfect for slashing, thrusting, and killing. It had a long wooden hilt and its users wielded it with both hands. Jesus brings up a sword here because governors in Pergamum had *the right of the sword*, or the power to carry out capital punishment. The governors were abusing this power in order to persecute Christians for posing a threat to their worship and worldview. This punishment was always the secular last word. But Christ reminded them that *He* was the one who would have the final word. The power of judgment was in *His* hands. In the end, Christ is going to speak and the rest of the world is going to have to accept what He says, like it or not.

This week, don't get discouraged because the culture has become so anti-God and the rhetoric so anti-Christ. While it certainly is demonic, Jesus is going to put things back in order when He has the final say. Until then, walk in love and keep your Facebook posts from getting out of hand. Keep them loving. It's crucial that you do.

PRAYER FOR THE WEEK

Dear Heavenly Father—
It bothers me to see how society has become so anti-You. Righteous liv-
ing is scoffed at and Your ways are being confused. But I thank You
that You will have the final say. I take confidence in knowing that all
of Your laws will prevail. Lord, fill me with the power of Your Spirit to
walk in the love of God as I preach the truth. In Jesus's name, amen!

ACTIVITY FOR THE WEEK

Cool off for a while on social media sites. Hold off on getting into an
argument. Instead of commenting, pray for the person you are ready to
challenge. Ask the Lord to open the eyes of their heart to see the truth.
(See Ephesians 1:17–18.) Pray that the Holy Spirit convicts them before
He has the final say. And just be loving.

SCRIPTURES FOR THE WEEK

1 Samuel 2:9–10	Proverbs 16:1
Psalm 2	2 Thessalonians 2:8
Psalm 28:2–4	Revelation 19:15

19

LIVING WITH THE DEVIL

I know where you dwell, where Satan's throne is.

(Revelation 2:13a)

Οἶδα ποῦ κατοικεῖς, ὅπου ὁ θρόνος τοῦ Σατανᾶ.

(ΑΠΟΚΑΛΥΨΙΣ ΙΩΑΝΝΟΥ 2:13a)

I'm packing up and leaving town. We're getting out of here as fast as we can."

You'd think a volcano was getting ready to erupt. When *I* heard those words, a minister was telling me that the Super Bowl was coming to town. Visitors from around the world were headed in for a time of unrestrained, old-fashioned hedonism. The minister had become so panic-stricken, he was packing up his car and getting out of Dodge. I think he felt like he was Lot getting out of Sodom. (See Genesis 19:14.) The only difference is Sodom was about to have a shower of fire and brimstone; this minister's city was not. On a positive note, his wife wasn't turned into a statue of salt.

While society's wickedness isn't something that should excite us, it isn't something that should make us fearful either. It's true that we are commanded to *run* from temptation (see 1 Corinthians 6:18), but this refers to not being docile in a moment of temptation. That's quite different from trying to escape your culture because it's wicked. As long as we are in this world, we are going to be surrounded by the darkness. If we're supposed to pack the car every time evil comes lurking, who would win this world to Christ? Jesus calls His church a lampstand, remember? (See Revelation 2:1.) We are to shine His light *into* the darkness. Nobody knew this better than the Pergamum church.

Right from the start, Jesus tells the Pergamum church He knows where they dwell. It just so happened to be the same place Satan inhabited. The Greek word for "dwell" is *katoikeō*. It means to have your permanent address somewhere: the place where your house is. For instance, I may stay in hotels while I am traveling, but my dwelling is in Michigan, USA. That's where my home is at the time of this writing. In fact, *katoikeō* is from the Greek word *oikos*, which means "house." Jesus was saying that the believers in Pergamum and the devil had houses on the same street. The Pergamum believers had a neighbor from hell!

> "Economics" comes from the Greek word "oikonomia" (*oikos* meaning "house" and *nemein* meaning "manage"). Economics is the management of resources from where we live and dwell.

If you've ever had bad neighbors, you know they can make life difficult. I had a neighbor who had *two* cocker spaniels. Cocker spaniels need a lot of attention or they will protest by barking in despair. I lived in a townhouse and the neighbor lived below me. When his garage door opened and I heard him leave, it was game on. I kid you not, those dogs once barked for four hours straight. But I didn't go outside and drive a "for sale" sign into the ground. I could have moved next door to someone who pounded on a drum set all night long. No matter where you go, there's always something.

CITY FILLED WITH DEMONIC ACTIVITY

Satan wasn't just the believers' neighbor; he was also their mayor. He had more than just a house in Pergamum; he had a throne. Thrones were large, opulent seats from which authority reigned. The words *"Satan's throne"* (*tou Satana ho thronos*) provide us detail in the Greek. Here, "Satan" (*tou Satana*) means that Satan was operating from his throne and it implies that demonic activity was prevalent and the norm.[22] Satan's tremendous spiritual influence in Pergamum resulted in all of the various expressions of idol worship, unclean ways of living, and the persecution of Christians.

Evil dwells in every city, with demonic activity going on. Wicked entities work from within to hold cities in darkness and tyrannize the truth. This is why some cities have gang violence and some have an abundance of contempt toward God. It's why some cities are infested with prostitution and why some are troubled by ongoing political corruption. Satan has deployed his wicked government all over the world and it works in every city to deter God's righteous ways. (See Ephesians 6:12.)

But here's the catch: your city needs you. It needs your church. It needs the people of God who are filled with the mighty Holy Spirit. And this is why God allows us to live in the same neighborhood as Satan. And it's the reason why you shouldn't move just because you hear the sound of something upsetting. Wickedness and righteousness are going to share space in this life. Like bickering roommates, they are going to have to live together until evil's lease is up. Then, Jesus will come and dethrone Satan and evict all wickedness. (See Revelation 21:1–4.) Until then, we need to shine the light no matter how dark the neighborhood might be.

Don't quit your job because you're the only Christian there. Don't divorce your unsaved spouse in hopes you'll find a Christian one. (See 1 Corinthians 7:10.) And, certainly, don't pack up when the Super Bowl comes to town. Instead, ask the Holy Spirit to fill you with His power and ability to witness so you can be a streetlight on your block.

PRAYER FOR THE WEEK

Dear Heavenly Father—
You know where I live, and You know that I am surrounded by evil.
But You have not given me the spirit of fear. You have given me a spirit
of power, love, and a sound mind, as You promise me in 2 Timothy
1:7. Fill me fresh with Your Holy Spirit so that the darkness around me

can be overcome with Your light in me. Open up divine opportunities for me to share the gospel so others can hear and be saved. Though the darkness might be much, great is Your light in me. Therefore, I never need to retreat in fear. In Jesus's name, amen!

ACTIVITY FOR THE WEEK

Shine your light and tell someone about Jesus. Ask the Lord to give you a divine opportunity—an obvious moment that begs for you to share the gospel. Then, take advantage of it by telling the individual you are ministering to about the love of Jesus and His power to deliver them from sin and the devil. Lastly, pray for and over that person. Bind the work of the devil in their life and lead them in the sinner's prayer to receive Jesus.

SCRIPTURES FOR THE WEEK

Matthew 5:13–16	Acts 1:8
Matthew 28:19	Acts 14:3
Mark 16:15–18	1 Peter 2:9

20

KEEP THE GAP WIDE

[I know where you dwell]…where Satan dwells.
(Revelation 2:13c)

[Οἶδα ποῦ κατοικεῖς]...ὅπου ὁ Σατανᾶς κατοικεῖ.
(ΑΠΟΚΑΛΥΨΙΣ ΙΩΑΝΝΟΥ 2:13c)

Are you a FaceTimer? Don't you just love hearing that whoosh when the person's face pops up on your phone? One minute, you're alone in a boring hotel; the next minute, it's your wife and child! Your bride beams with delight: eyebrows arched, cheeks stretched, and a smile that spans from Burbank to Boston. And, of course, your little baby girl scrunches her face in confusion, wondering how daddy got into the little plastic box.

People love FaceTime because much of communication is nonverbal. You know, our expressions: winks, nods, and scratches on our chin. Believe it or not, God's Word contains these. They are found in what is known as implicit commentary, communication that's not specifically stated in words. John was known for doing this. Often, he would wink at his readers in hopes they might read between the lines. One way he did this was through clever placement of words and phrases. Revelation 2:13 provides a good example.

Here, Jesus says, *"I know where you dwell"* (*oida pou katoikeis*). The verse continues into Christ's message to the believers in Pergamum. It describes the problems and persecution that Satan was causing them and then closes with *"where Satan dwells"* (*ho Satanas katoikei*). Notice something here: the letter opens by emphasizing who dwells in Pergamum, both Christians and Satan. And there's a clash in the middle. Jesus was drawing a picture. It's a tug of war: Christians on one side, Satan on the other. And in between them, tension—lots and lots of tension. This is a non-verbal cue that although Christians and Satan live together, they'll always stand on opposite sides.

There should be a large degree of separation between Christians and the devil; Satan hates the church and the church detests Satan. It needs to stay this way. Jesus reminds us that we should never attempt to take sides with the enemy. People should never observe the way we talk and act and see that gap getting smaller. There needs to be plenty of space and plenty of tension within that space.

WORLD IS FULL OF ENTICEMENTS

While it is unfathomable to think of taking sides with Satan himself, people side with Satan when they buddy up to the world. (See 1 John 2:15.) All too often this happens because there are plenty of enticements in the world that make it attractive. (See 1 John 2:16.) First, there are those selfish desires that come from the flesh: talking about others behind their backs, lying to get out of trouble, materialism, sexting, treating your spouse cruelly, and gluttony. Then, there are those things that draw us from afar: craving to be YouTube famous, obsessing over Bitcoin, going into debt just to have a designer outfit, and being a workaholic. Finally, there is pride that comes from being in love with ourselves for who we are and what we've done: attributing our success to ourselves instead of God, ingratitude, entitlement, conceit, and self-importance. God's Word calls all of these the desires of the flesh, the desires of the eyes, and the pride of life. When we move in the direction of these things, we move in the direction of Satan.

As Christians, we must be cautious. These things are trendy because our culture is under the influence of the devil. (See 2 Corinthians 4:4.) If we give more devotion to the culture than we do to God's Word, the gap between us and the devil is certain to get smaller.

The Brazen Bull was one of the worst torture devices ever created. It was an all-brass statue, the size of an actual bull, and hollow inside. Victims were tied up and placed within, then a fire was kindled underneath to roast the victim inside. Pipes built within the bull converted the victims' scream into sounds that sounded like grunts and snorts, making the bull seem alive to those watching from outside.

Instead, we need to be like Antipas, who was a martyr from the church in Pergamum. History tells us that he was sealed inside a huge bull made of brass and burned alive. He gave his life instead of compromising Christ to conform to the culture. What's interesting is his name. It's a two-part Greek word: *anti* which means "against" and *pas* which means "all." Against all, *Antipas* stood his ground against the allure of the other side. He kept the gap wide and kept the tension tight.

How big is the gap between you and our culture? Are you flirting with trends or are you faithful to God's truth? Like Antipas, resolve that, this week, you are going to stand against all the things that the world says are "in." When they start tugging at you, dig your feet further into the ground and declare you aren't going to budge. You're on the winning side already. It's not worth it to give up.

PRAYER FOR THE WEEK

Dear Heavenly Father—
Thank You that You have placed me on Your side and separated me from the world. You are my Lord, not the culture in which I live. Holy Spirit, fill my heart with a love for truth and not trends. Give me Your

strength to stand against all the enticements of Satan that are so prevalent in society today. I declare that I am on the winning side and, because I stand my ground, You honor me with blessings and everlasting life. In Jesus's name, amen!

ACTIVITY FOR THE WEEK

Draw two vertical lines down a piece of paper so it's divided into three columns. Label the first column side "God's Side," the middle column "My Life," and the third column "Satan's Side." List all of your habits, interests, and actions under the middle column labeled My Life. Now, draw a line from each activity and connect it either God's Side or Satan's Side. You now have a picture of your ways. Are you uncompromising like Antipas? Or are there some things you need to ask the Holy Spirit to help you to change?

SCRIPTURES FOR THE WEEK

Exodus 32:26

Joshua 24:15

Micah 4:5

Matthew 6:24–25

James 4:4

1 John 2:15–17

21

AN OPPORTUNITY TO WALK AWAY

Yet you hold fast my name, and you did not deny my faith even in the days of Antipas my faithful witness, who was killed among you, where Satan dwells. (Revelation 2:13b)

καὶ κρατεῖς τὸ ὄνομά μου καὶ οὐκ ἠρνήσω τὴν πίστιν μου καὶ ἐν ταῖς ἡμέραις Ἀντιπᾶς ὁ μάρτυς μου ὁ πιστός μου, ὃς ἀπεκτάνθη παρ' ὑμῖν. (ΑΠΟΚΑΛΥΨΙΣ ΙΩΑΝΝΟΥ 2:13b)

For over two decades, the "Lakehouse" was our family's retreat from the stale air of congested suburban life. Located in Mears, Michigan, it sat on four sandy acres between Silver Lake and Lake Michigan. The oxygen was crisp and pure, saturated with damp hints of cedar, pine, and surf. Our blood danced as we savored the breath of it. At night, the sky turned into a black platter featuring celestial delicacies that our eyes feasted on without restraint. The cricket nation serenaded us all evening. Going to bed was the nightcap. Our pillows were cool and dense, wafting the aroma of the clean country air. If there were ever a moment one was certain that nothing was an accident, that one was in the center of the Creator's sovereign plan, it was at the Lakehouse. It's no wonder the vintage, wood-burned sign on the porch read, "Almost Heaven."

Not every day is a Lakehouse day. There are some days that make you feel as though your head has been dropped into a blender that's pureeing strawberries for a smoothie. Your beliefs are whipped back and forth by the blades of life and your reasoning is pressed for everything life contains. Discombobulated and despairing, there's a temptation to question the plans of God. Ask God's greatest prophets; they knew what it felt like. (See, for example, Jeremiah 12:1–4.)

Take 9/11—September 11, 2001. Do you remember where you were when you heard that planes had smashed into the World Trade Center's Twin Towers and the Pentagon? How did you process the deaths of nearly three thousand innocent people of all ages and from all walks of life?

If you haven't yet been to college, be prepared: your atheist professors will use tragic current events to make salsa out of you. They will ask you, "If there was a God, would He let this happen?" Christ-rejecters and God-despisers will use every circumstance about which you are uncertain to refute every instance where you've been certain. They will try to ruin your Lakehouse moments by pointing to 9/11. Or mass shootings. Or the Holocaust. And you will have a choice: hold on to God or disassociate yourself from Him.

OUR FAITH BRINGS PRAISE

The believers in Pergamum were given the same choice under comparable circumstances. It's certain that they had experienced a genuine conversion to Christ. But a tragedy had befallen their community: Antipas had been brutally martyred. There was nothing consoling about his death. In light of this event, Jesus says, *"Yet you hold fast my name, and you did not deny my faith"* (kai krateis to onoma mou kai ouk erneso tēn pistin mou).

There are a few interesting things to observe in the Greek. First, the verb here for "deny" (ērnēsō) means to disassociate from something and deny that it is true. It is found in a manner that emphasizes a very specific instance.[23] When Antipas was killed, the church was faced with a precise chance to disassociate themselves from Jesus. Understandably, they had unanswered questions, difficulty understanding, and even faced pressure from unbelievers to stop serving their "cult" and get with the rest of society.

The next thing we see about this statement is that it is an antithesis, which emphasizes a declaration by stating a negative version of the same statement. For instance: "I am full; I am not hungry." Or "My life is great; it couldn't be better." The negative statement serves to reinforce the initial positive statement. It adds emphasis and weight. Jesus was saying, "You held fast to your faith and *that's* a big deal! Well done!"

One of the best-selling books of all time, *A Tale of Two Cities* by Charles Dickens, opens with a striking antithesis: "It was the best of times, it was the worst of times..." Antitheses grip our interest and keep us reading further.

When the Pergamum believers were faced with the wide-open opportunity to walk away from Jesus due to the tragic and inexplicable event, they instead hunkered down. It wasn't a "let's just see how it goes for a few more days" kind of attitude. It was a firm and solid determination that their heartbreak and lack of answers couldn't change the reality they had experienced in Christ. And, for this, Christ commends them.

Looking back on my own life, I remember the *exact* moments when I had opportunities to deny my faith. Like the time when I was in college, standing on Hennepin Avenue in Minneapolis, talking to a group of atheists who made a convincing case against the justice and sovereignty of God. Despite their best attacks, I held tight to what I held to be true. Can you remember exact moments when you had to hold tight to your faith so it didn't get away?

There will be a specific instance in life where you are going to be given a chance to disassociate yourself from everything you've experienced in Christ. It may occur when tragedy strikes or it could take place after a fancy, "enlightening" lecture. It might happen if you become famous or go broke. Whatever the cause may be, you can be sure that the blades of life will try to shred your Lakehouse experiences. Will you become unfaithful to Jesus because you don't have *all* the answers? Or will you draw closer to Him for the answers He *has* given you to hold onto? Don't think God doesn't see or appreciate the times you have to fight to hold onto your faith in Him. He does—and it's a big deal to Him.

PRAYER FOR THE WEEK

Dear Heavenly Father—
I may not have all the answers to life's most difficult questions, but I have experienced times wherein You've revealed Yourself to me. I thank You for those precious times when the Holy Spirit has assured me that You are and You will always be. When the enemy tries to sway my faith with doubt, I pray You strengthen me like the believers in Pergamum so that I may ground myself even deeper in the truth. I declare I will be a believer until I see You face to face. In Jesus's name, amen!

ACTIVITY FOR THE WEEK

Focus on every *answer* God has ever given to you. Make a list of all the instances where God has spoken to you and assured you that He is present and active in your life. Pick one that is curiously peculiar and has God's fingerprints all over it. Journal about it. What made it so peculiar? What was God saying to you in this? How can you use this when believing becomes a challenge?

SCRIPTURES FOR THE WEEK

Job 1:22	2 Timothy 2:11–13
Mark 8:38	2 Timothy 3:14–15
2 Timothy 1:8, 13–14	Titus 1:9, 15–16

22

INDIFFERENCE CAUSES FIRES

But I have a few things against you: you have some there who hold the teaching of Balaam, who taught Balak to put a stumbling block before the sons of Israel, so that they might eat food sacrificed to idols and practice sexual immorality.

(Revelation 2:14)

ἀλλ' ἔχω κατὰ σοῦ ὀλίγα ὅτι ἔχεις ἐκεῖ κρατοῦντας τὴν διδαχὴν Βαλαάμ, ὃς ἐδίδασκεν τῷ Βαλὰκ βαλεῖν σκάνδαλον ἐνώπιον τῶν υἱῶν Ἰσραὴλ φαγεῖν εἰδωλόθυτα καὶ πορνεῦσαι. (ΑΠΟΚΑΛΥΨΙΣ ΙΩΑΝΝΟΥ 2:14)

The year 1666 provides us with one of the rawest displays of indifference that the world has ever known. London was recovering after the Great

Plague. It didn't seem like things could get any worse. That is, until Thomas Farriner's bakery on Pudding Lane went up in flames. In those days, a single blaze was a threat to a whole city because houses and buildings were made out of wood. The right wind could swiftly turn the city into an inferno.

London's mayor, Sir Thomas Bloodworth, was indifferent about the fire's potential. He crudely remarked that a woman could urinate on it and put it out. Three hundred houses soon caught fire. By the next day, half of London was ablaze. At one point, firefighters hoped to create a break in the fire's path so they used gunpowder to blow up houses along the trajectory of the inferno. When the blasts were heard, a rumor spread that the French had come to seize the city. Terror mushroomed.

The mess lasted four days. By the time it cooled, four-fifths of London— including 13,000 homes, 89 churches, and every municipal building—had been destroyed. Things would have been *different* if Mayor Bloodworth hadn't been *indifferent*.

Indifference is a lack of interest or concern. It appears in our society every day. Litterbugs, the person who always shows up late, or the road menace who ignores everyone else's safety by texting while they drive. When we ignore the things we shouldn't, we end up getting burned. This was the case in Pergamum.

In Revelation 2:13, Jesus wraps up his commendation to the believers with criticism. He makes His problem with them very clear: *"You have some there who hold to the teaching of Balaam"* (*echeis ekei kratountas tēn didachēn Balaam*). The Greek word for "you have" (*echeis*) means to *have right now, at this moment,* and it implies having no intention of giving it up.[24] The Pergamum church had people in their congregation who were following the teaching of Balaam and the leadership had zero intention of getting rid of them. They planned to keep them in their congregation. And Jesus had an issue with this.

Balaam was a false prophet from the Old Testament. His name tells us everything we need to know. It's a two-part name of Hebrew origin: *bala* (he swallows) and *'am* (people). Put it together and you get a prophet who swallows up the people.

In Numbers 24, Balaam advised Balak, king of the Moabites, how to defeat Israel. If Israel began to worship idols, they would lose God's protection. So, Balaam counseled the Moabite women to entice the men of Israel to engage in sexual immorality with them. (See Numbers 25:1.) Soon afterward, the Israelite men began to worship Moabite idols and lost God's favor.

From that time forward, Balaam represented false teachers who enticed God's people to relax their standards and make allowances for unclean behavior and sin. (See Numbers 31:16.) And there were those in the Pergamum church who were listening to teachers like Balaam and living the same loose lives.

INDIFFERENCE IS A STUMBLING BLOCK

The leadership in Pergamum was indifferent about it. Maybe they were afraid of confrontation, or perhaps they didn't want to offend the culture. Perhaps they felt getting along was more important than regard for what God considers holy.

Jesus sets the record straight. He refers to their unclean living as a *"stumbling block"* (*skandalon*). This word referred to the part on a trap where bait is positioned. When touched, the trap snaps on the victim. Loose living is a trap. Anyone walking carelessly around it is certain to get entangled. Jesus was upset at the Pergamum church because they were indifferent about their people walking under the trap. Instead of rebuking them, the believers in Pergamum tolerated them. When sin gets near God's people, God expects His people to do something about it. Otherwise, someone is going to get burned or caught in a trap.

> The English word "scandal" comes from the Greek word *skandalon* ("stumbling block" or "trap"). A scandal is an action or event that causes outrage and anger. It begins when the offender is coerced into sin and wrongdoing.

God doesn't want compromise with culture in our lives, our homes, or our churches. As Christians, we are supposed to have made a clean break from what the culture tells us is "normative" and acceptable. Christians are most often referred to in the Bible as "saints" or "holy ones" (*hagios*). (See Romans 1:7.) This means those who look "different" from the world.

Does your choice of TV shows and movies look different? How about your Internet history? What about your text conversations? Everything compromising that we have—and have no plans to get rid of—needs to go. If it doesn't, it could whirl into a blaze. Thank God that He wakes us up before the fire gets out of control. Is God waking you up about something? Will you be indifferent, or will you ask Him for His help to put out the fire?

PRAYER FOR THE WEEK

Dear Heavenly Father—
I don't want to be indifferent toward the things that displease and dishonor You. When I made You the Lord of my life, You filled me with the presence of the Holy Spirit. May the things that alarm You, alarm me. Should compromise enter my presence, give me the discernment to detect it and the boldness to put it out. May my words, thoughts, actions, and conversations be acceptable unto You. In Jesus's name, amen!

ACTIVITY FOR THE WEEK

Set an alarm on your phone for a random time in the middle of the day this week. Each day it goes off, ask the Lord to search your life. Let the Holy Spirit examine how you are spending your day. Are there any fires you need to put out? Before you move on with your day, thank God for His holiness that resides in your life.

SCRIPTURES FOR THE WEEK

1 Corinthians 5:11–13	1 John 4:1
Ephesians 4:17–24	2 John 7–11
Colossians 3:5–6	Jude 19–21

23

GOD'S CUTTING WORDS ARE FOR YOUR OWN GOOD

Therefore repent. If not, I will come to you soon and war against them with the sword of my mouth. (Revelation 2:16)

μετανόησον οὖν· εἰ δὲ μή, ἔρχομαί σοι ταχὺ καὶ πολεμήσω μετ᾽ αὐτῶν ἐν τῇ ῥομφαίᾳ τοῦ στόματός μου.
(ΑΠΟΚΑΛΥΨΙΣ ΙΩΑΝΝΟΥ 2:16)

Rarely does a best-selling Amazon product with a thousand five-star reviews disappoint. This time, I had ordered a fancy kitchen knife set and was anxious to see what the blades could do. I decided it would be best to try them out "infomercial style," so I positioned the cutlery up on the counter and began chucking vegetables its way. When that got boring, I minced up some pennies and deboned a rotisserie chicken. It was like a real late-night promotional, minus the invisible, fast-talking guy who tells you at the end to *order now!* Nothing was slowing my pace...that is, until my hand slipped off and ended up in the knife's ravenous path. My eyes crossed, my face went pale, and I let out a yelp the penguins in Antarctica heard a few hours later. My infomercial had come to an end. I shouldn't have been fooling around to begin with. I haven't played with a set of knives since. If you've ever been stung by a blade, you know as well as I, it has the power to get your attention and stop you from messing around.

> The *rhomphaia* was one of the most feared weapons on the ancient battlefield. Its pole-arm design gave extended range and its curved blade allowed users to slash, thrust, or hack with ease. Opponents had to add extra reinforcement to their helmets to protect against its blows.

JESUS HAS SHARP WORDS FOR US

The Pergamum church had been careless. They were fooling around with teaching that enabled loose living. In Revelation 2:16, Jesus attempts to get their attention with a sharp blade of His own: His Word. Here, Jesus refers to this blade as *"the sword of my mouth"* (*te rhomphaia mou stomatos*). The way this phrase is set up is interesting: His sword *is* His mouth.[25] Jesus's words are like a set of knives that are sharp enough to pierce us and make us stop to consider what we've been doing. Have you ever had a moment in your life when you were getting carried away with something foolish and, suddenly, God spoke to you and made you think twice? This is called conviction. Conviction is a word from God that keeps us from continuing in the wrong direction. It often stings. But taking heed will safeguard our soul.

Jesus's word of conviction to the believers in Pergamum was *"Therefore repent."* The Greek word "therefore" (*oun*) tells what Jesus concluded about the whole matter.[26] They needed to "repent" or "re-think" their attitude toward sin.

Notice, conviction isn't a long instruction. It's straight and to the point. When Jesus convicts, it's so simple that it's hard to mistake it. It usually isn't a forty-five-minute prophecy, a two-hour sermon, or pages and pages of prophetic revelation. It's often just a few extremely sharp words that we understand very clearly.

Jesus told the Pergamum church that it was critical for them to heed the conviction they were experiencing; otherwise, they would end up like Balaam. In Numbers 31:8, we read that Balaam was killed by a sword. Jesus is telling the Pergamum church something profound: when we heed His word, there is life, but when we disobey it, there is death. The sting of the Lord's conviction comes to keep us from experiencing more profound pain, especially the pain of missing out on eternal life.

Our twenty-first century culture thinks just about *everything* is right as long as it is *right for you*. This post-modern approach to morality is certain never to convict. And because it cannot convict, it can never save someone from the sorrows of sin and the consequences of breaking God's law. Culture will let you keep moving further and further from the Lord without ever saying a word. At the very least, Jesus will say something first, like "re-think—repent." He loves you too much to see sin carry you into captivity. He's not concerned that your feelings may be hurt by what you hear. He wants to see you inherit eternal life. And so, the Lord pierces us with the words of His mouth, in hopes that we think twice about how it feels to be in pain…or put someone else through pain.

Is there something in your life that the Lord has convicted you about? Maybe you've been listening to teaching that will corrupt your faith. Perhaps you've been seeking something—or working toward a specific goal—with the wrong motive. Maybe you are hurting someone and need to stop. It's possible you've even been living a numbed life, plodding through each day with a sad fatalism, waiting for the weekend, or even during the weekend.

Take heed to the Lord's conviction. His sharp words are for your own good. They may save your life or someone else's life. Or better yet, they may just save your soul.

PRAYER FOR THE WEEK

Dear Heavenly Father—
I thank You that You love me so much that You convict me. When
I am headed off course, Your words put me back on. You are not a

God who sugarcoats everything You say. Sometimes You give the blunt truth. But I thank You that You do everything in love with my best interest at heart. So today, I ask You to convict me when You see fit. As You do, I ask You for the help of the Holy Spirit to help me obey so I can keep living unto You. In Jesus's name, amen!

ACTIVITY FOR THE WEEK

Carefully carve your name into a tree. As you do, consider how God's Word works. Notice how sharp the blade is. Notice how the tree doesn't resist the knife. Is God's Word this effective when it brings conviction to your life? Do you let it have its way? Or do you resist?

SCRIPTURES FOR THE WEEK

Jeremiah 23:29	Ephesians 6:17
Hosea 6:5	2 Timothy 3:16
John 16:8–11	Hebrews 4:12

24

REJECTION MAKES A NAME

He who has an ear, let him hear what the Spirit says to the churches. To the one who conquers I will give some of the hidden manna, and I will give him a white stone, with a new name written on the stone that no one knows except the one who receives it. (Revelation 2:17)

ὁ ἔχων οὖς ἀκουσάτω τί τὸ πνεῦμα λέγει ταῖς ἐκκλησί-αις. τῷ νικῶντι δώσω αὐτῷ τοῦ μάννα τοῦ κεκρυμμένου καὶ δώσω αὐτῷ ψῆφον λευκήν, καὶ ἐπὶ τὴν ψῆφον ὄνομα καινὸν γεγραμμένον ὃ οὐδεὶς οἶδεν εἰ μὴ ὁ λαμβάνων.
(ΑΠΟΚΑΛΥΨΙΣ ΙΩΑΝΝΟΥ 2:17)

Bookstores are castles. Each shelf is a throne the authors have taken by conquest, having staked their name thereon. No book is enthroned upon a shelf before overcoming a starving journey, laden with loneliness, disappointment, and lots of rejection. Don't believe it? Dr. Seuss's first children's book, *And to Think That I Saw It on Mulberry Street*, was rejected twenty-seven times. Stephen King's *Carrie* had thirty rejections. And perhaps the greatest bout of rejection of all time is Jack Canfield and Mark Victor Hansen's *Chicken Soup for the Soul*—a whopping 144 rejections!

The royals of writing have earned their thrones and are well deserving of their rule in the land of bookstores. But before they ever got a name, their names were rejected…over…and over…again…and again. They weren't always accepted as they are today. That should give one a new appreciation for writing and what it takes to earn a name.

In Revelation 2:17, Jesus attaches rejection to the price of a name. The Lord had made His intolerance for compromise known to the Pergamum church. They knew their time for walking the line had come to an end. Choosing to accept God's Word was going to result in rejection from the world. Jesus knew it would not be an easy road. But Jesus is faithful. He gives them an incentive to strengthen their faith. He promises that He will reward them with the hidden manna (eternal life), as well as a white stone with a new name.

A white stone with your new name inscribed upon it! This would have excited the believers. It would have been a marvelous promise to their ears and would have encouraged them that the road ahead was worthwhile. It would have been the equivalent of a publisher telling Dr. Seuss that he was going to be published. A promise like that is enough to keep someone going!

So, what were the stones? The Greek word is *psēphos*, which was a rare word to use. The more common Greek word is *lithos*, which is used many times throughout the New Testament. *Psēphos* is only used one other time in the New Testament outside of this verse. This indicates that it had a very specific purpose.

The *psēphos* was also used in voting. Within the courtroom, jurors would drop their pebble into one of two urns, one representing condemnation and the other representing acquittal. Today, the study of voting is called "psephology."

FREE TICKETS TO THE GREAT FEAST

During the days of the Roman Empire, there were certain times when the government handed out free admission to games and events, along with free food. Imagine your city council or county government giving everyone a free ticket to a festival or concert, plus free refreshments. You might get a bright pink ticket that said *TICKET* on the back. But they didn't have those in the Roman Empire. Instead, they used a special white stone or a *psēphos*. These stones often had the individual's name on them. Hence, the stones represented admission and acceptance into a feast. Jesus was inviting the believers to share in the glory of His eternal kingdom. Although society wanted nothing to do with the Christians, Jesus had handed them an admission ticket and asking them to come to *His* party.

Though many governments in our world reject those who follow Jesus, the King of Kings issues a ticket to all who love Him and hold onto His name.

In addition, Jesus promises that each person who is admitted will receive a new name that no one else will know except the one to whom it is given. The Greek word "new" is *kainos*. This means "unused, superior in value, and impressive." *Kainos* would describe a brand new, limited-edition, custom-made Ferrari—the only one of its kind. Think of the value! That's *kainos*. God has a *kainos* name just for you.

On home fixer-upper shows, sometimes the person who is getting a new house asks the designers to incorporate something sentimental from their old house, like a tile or a table. This puts character into the new home and makes it unique from any other home on the block.

Our new name will be unknown to others because it's made up of our personal sufferings, unique to us. It incorporates all of those hard moments when we were rejected for the name of Christ. God saw that rejection and He made a name out of it for you. Before you get a name from Christ, you have to be rejected by the world.

If it just so happens that you have a hard time this week because of the ways of the world, remember Christ is using the rejection to make a custom name for you that will give you admittance to His eternal feast. There's a lot ahead to look forward to. Don't let some heckling from the world cause you to get down. Your name is being made by God and He is going to issue a ticket for you into His eternal kingdom.

PRAYER FOR THE WEEK

Dear Heavenly Father—
It is a privilege when the world rejects me for Your name. You are taking all of this rejection and using it to make a name out of it for me in heaven. Therefore, I will be joyful in tribulations because I know You have accepted me into Your eternal kingdom. What a joy it is to be accepted by You. Holy Spirit, I pray that You continually remind me this week just how accepted I am in Christ. In Jesus's name, amen!

ACTIVITY FOR THE WEEK

Buy a roll of pink raffle tickets. Write your name on a few and place them everywhere you commonly look throughout the week, such as in the refrigerator, on the mirror, in your wallet, and on the kitchen counter. When you see a ticket, hold it up in the air and say, "Thank You, Father, that because of Jesus, *You* have accepted me. It doesn't matter that the world rejects me. I am coming to *Your* party!"

SCRIPTURES FOR THE WEEK

Luke 14:12–24	Hebrews 3:6, 14
John 14:1–4	Hebrews 10:23
1 Corinthians 1:9	1 Peter 1:3–4

PART V

THE CHURCH AT THYATIRA—STUDIES ON HOLINESS

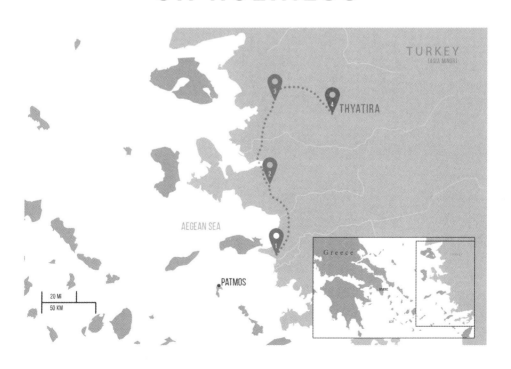

25

JESUS: HOMEBOY OR HOLY HOMEBOY?

And to the angel of the church in Thyatira write: The words of the Son of God, who has eyes like a flame of fire, and whose feet are like burnished bronze. (Revelation 2:18)

Καὶ τῷ ἀγγέλῳ τῆς ἐν Θυατείροις ἐκκλησίας γράψον Τάδε λέγει ὁ υἱὸς τοῦ θεοῦ, ὁ ἔχων τοὺς ὀφθαλμοὺς αὐτοῦ ὡς φλόγα πυρὸς καὶ οἱ πόδες αὐτοῦ ὅμοιοι χαλκολιβάνῳ. (ΑΠΟΚΑΛΥΨΙΣ ΙΩΑΝΝΟΥ 2:18)

In 2004, the movie *Passion of the Christ*[27] cleaned up at the box office, making $83.8 million on its opening weekend and clearing nearly $612 million worldwide. It also created a resurgence in interest in Jesus. If you were at least a teenager back then, I'm certain you remember the trendy

"Jesus Is My Homeboy" T-shirt craze. Everyone was wearing them, from kids to pastors to A-list celebrities like Brad Pitt, Jessica Simpson, and Pamela Anderson. You couldn't go to a mall without spotting one.

The T-shirt's creator was Van Zan Frater[28], who was mugged by a gang in the 1980s in southcentral Los Angeles. They beat him up, pulled a gun on him, and were about to send a bullet into his skull when he shouted, "Jesus is my homeboy!" The gang stood down and Zan Frater walked away with his life. He designed the shirt to get out the message.

By the mid-2000s, most people wearing the shirts didn't know the backstory. In fact, Zan Frater wasn't even printing the shirts at that time. A fashion designer found one of his old shirts in a thrift store and began using it, thinking it would sell well.

While I agree with Zan Frater's message in light of the backstory, I was concerned about the trend. Did the people who were wearing the T-shirt know what the message was? Sure, some connected it to similar instances in their life. But did most?

According to urbandictionary.com, a "homeboy" is "a person you always chill with." That's what most of culture thought it meant: "Jesus chills with me." It creates the idea that Jesus isn't a lame friend who spoils our fun at a party. We're not perfect and He hangs with us anyway. He isn't a tattle who tells our parents we're smoking weed behind the school. He may even fire one up with us and talk about life.

Yet this isn't how Jesus describes Himself to the church of Thyatira. Quite the opposite actually.

Thyatira is the smallest of the seven churches addressed in Revelation 2–3. The ironic thing is that Jesus devotes His longest letter to it. The church was small but they had *big* problems. To understand these problems, it's important to know that Thyatira was a center for manufacturing and trade. They had trade guilds for metal workers, bronze-smiths, leather workers, and others. If a person had a trade, it was vital that they join their guild and be with other craftsmen who had mutual goals. It's like being a pastor and belonging to a ministerial association or being a golfer and belonging to a country club.

JESUS HAS HIGHER STANDARDS

Obviously, the believers in the church in Thyatira had trades and would need to join guilds. The problem was, the guilds were often dedicated to pagan gods. When the guilds had events and celebrations, all members needed to attend. At these festivals, food was offered to the gods and acts of repulsive perversion took place. The believers in Thyatira were faced with a choice: would Jesus be their homeboy and come chill with them at the party (as long as they didn't do *all* the bad things, of course)? Or did Jesus have another standard He expected them to abide by?

In Revelation 2:18, Jesus reveals Himself to the Thyatrians as *"the Son of God, who has eyes like a flame of fire, and whose feet are like burnished bronze."* This is the only place in Revelation that Jesus is called the Son of God. It is placed here because Apollo was the chief deity worshipped in Thyatira. He was the son of the chief god, Zeus. The term "the Son of God" (*ho huios tou theou*) is used in a way that makes it obvious that God is the Father of Jesus, and Jesus is His Son.[29] The term stood as a claim that *only* Jesus is the Son of God, not the false god Apollo.

It also means that Jesus had different standards. Unlike Apollo, Jesus was absolutely holy. This is found in the Greek word "has" (*echōn*): He *has* eyes that burn like flames and *has* feet that shimmer like bronze. This sets the record straight about Jesus.[30] He is not like the Jesus we see on the "Jesus Is My Homeboy" T-shirts. He is the glorified Jesus who sits on His throne in heaven.

> Suidas, a tenth century author who wrote the Suida, an encyclopedia about the ancient Greek world, said burnished bronze, *chalkolibanō*, was more precious than gold.

His eyes of fire represent His fierceness toward sin (see Daniel 10:6) and His shimmering bronze feet represent his unmatched holiness. This is explained by the Greek word for "burnished bronze" (*chalkolibanō*). It refers to a remarkable bronze alloy that had unmatched purity. He was sending the Thyatrians a message that He wouldn't oblige them if they chose to sin. The true Son of God walks in holiness and moves in virtue. He despises sin and can't live among it.

Jesus may be your homeboy if you're being robbed, but He'll never be your homeboy when you indulge in sin. He can't; He's holy. This week, tell Jesus He is more than a homeboy to you. Tell Him He is the true and holy Son of God, your "Holy Homeboy." When you have that revelation of Him, it's certain you'll live in reverence and awe of Him, instead of just seeing Him as another one of your buddies. Then, you can walk alongside Him in holiness and strength.

PRAYER FOR THE WEEK

Dear Heavenly Father—
Lord, You are holy, and it is my desire to be holy just like You. I ask You to cleanse me and purify me with Your fire. Burn away anything that separates us. Holy Spirit, I desire to honor You with my body, mind, and spirit. Therefore, I will not give place to sin nor will I allow it entry into my life. In Jesus's name, amen!

ACTIVITY FOR THE WEEK

Buy a new pair of socks and wear them outdoors with no shoes. Journal about it. How did it make you feel? Did you feel out of place? Uncomfortable? Did it bother you that the socks were so dirty afterward? The next time you are tempted to sin, this will remind you that Jesus walks only in purity...and so should we.

SCRIPTURES FOR THE WEEK

Isaiah 6:1–5	Matthew 17:1–5
Ezekiel 10:4	Mark 1:24
Daniel 7:9–10	Revelation 20:11

26

LOVE IS HOLINESS

I know your works, your love and faith and service and patient endurance, and that your latter works exceed the first.

(Revelation 2:19)

Οἶδά σου τὰ ἔργα καὶ τὴν ἀγάπην καὶ τὴν πίστιν καὶ τὴν διακονίαν καὶ τὴν ὑπομονήν σου, καὶ τὰ ἔργα σου τὰ ἔσχατα πλείονα τῶν πρώτων.

(ΑΠΟΚΑΛΥΨΙΣ ΙΩΑΝΝΟΥ 2:19)

There's an old-fashioned directive that preachers like to use. First, they tell their congregations to take someone by the hand and shake it like they are going to shake their arm loose. While everyone is shaking and the room is quaking, the band starts playing and the organ starts howling, and the preacher says: "Now tell your neighbor: 'Neighbor! I may not be all that I *want* to be. But thank God I'm not what I *used* to be. And because of

Jesus, I'm getting *better* every day!'" One hundred times out of a hundred, the people shout, the band turns it up, and there's a praise break. Such excitement!

Every day one lives is a day to become more like God. That's the epitome of holiness. And, *that's* something to get turned up about.

Holiness is simply living like God. (See 1 Peter 2:9.) In spite of the problems going on in the church in Thyatira, there were those who had grown in holiness and had become more like God. Jesus was excited about it and acknowledges it. He says, *"Your latter works exceed the first"* (*sou ta eschata ta erga pleiona tōn prōtōn*). This means that Jesus is comparing the believers in Thyatira to what they used to be. He finds that their works toward Him are mightier and more in number.[31] In other words, they now look more like God than when they first got saved. They had forgiven each other for stuff. They had stopped gossiping. They weren't cussing. They dumped out the booze. They threw away their drugs and stopped lying. They were serving at church. They weren't what they used to be and each day was getting better! If you had walked into the church, you'd have been pretty impressed by what you saw. It was a mature church with veteran Christians.

> The Agapanthus, also known as the African lily, is a beautiful flower indigenous to southern Africa. The name comes from the Greek words *agape* ("love") and *anthos* ("flower"). It means "a lovely flower." It's used to treat inflammation, heart disease, coughs, and paralysis.

JESUS COMMENDS US FOR OUR LOVE

The Thyatrians had become like God in four *major* areas: love (*agape*), faith (*pistis*), service (*diakonia*), and patient endurance (*hypomonē*)—listed in that order. Here, it's important to realize that the Greek language really takes advantage of word order to emphasize words. The closer a word is to the beginning of a sentence, the more important it usually is. Hence, Jesus places the most emphasis on the Thyatrians' growth in love. Before Jesus commends them for their mighty acts of faith, their hard works of service, and their unwavering endurance, He tips His hat toward their love.

Why the emphasis on this? Because God *is* love. (See 1 John 4:8.) It is the center of who He is. Everything God does, He does from love. Therefore, loving like God stands at the center of being like Him; it is the nucleus of holiness. Think about it. Love will end your road rage. It will shut your gossip column down at church. It will make *you* take the first step toward burying the hatchet with that arrogant relative of yours. It will keep you from cheating on your spouse. In fact, it will even keep you from doing any harm to yourself. When God sees you loving others, He sees you acting the way He would act and it reminds Him of Himself. When I walk in love with those around me, I imagine God thinks, "Attaboy. He's just like His daddy."

My dad has always been a cologne wearer. He actually puts cologne on before he goes to sleep. When I got my first cologne set, what do you think I began to do? My dad saw me one night, smiled, and said, "You know, you're just like your father." A father always takes notice when his child behaves like him. When you demonstrate love to others, even in the face of adversity, God recognizes where you got it—and He commends it.

It takes time to grow in holiness and God knows it. It happens little by little. This week, there will be opportunities for you to walk in love. Will you take advantage of them? You'll become more like the Father if you do and you'll be glad you did. You'll be able to say, "I am becoming better every day!"

PRAYER FOR THE WEEK

Dear Heavenly Father—
I thank You that I can be holy and walk in love just like You. Holy Spirit, help me to take advantage of each opportunity that comes along. I will not give in to my flesh, and I will not be ruled by my emotions. Instead, I will be like You—even if it's difficult. I'm putting the love of God first, each and every day…and my life will get better every day. In Jesus's name, amen!

ACTIVITY FOR THE WEEK

Keep a "Love Log." Every time there is an opportunity to walk in God's love this week, log it. This may include paying for the car behind you in a fast-food drive-through, putting coins in parking meters that aren't yours, sending someone an encouraging text, praying for someone in line at the store, or turning down a chance to gossip. List the occurrence, the date, time, and where it took place. Put a green check mark next to it if you seized the opportunity to walk in God's love; place a red "x" next to it if you didn't. At the end of the week, look at the green check marks compared to the red "x" marks. Have you grown in love? What will you do differently next week?

SCRIPTURES FOR THE WEEK

Deuteronomy 18:13	John 13:35
Leviticus 20:7–8	Ephesians 5:1
Matthew 5:43–48	1 Peter 1:16

27

QUARANTINE EVIL

But I have this against you, that you tolerate that woman Jezebel, who calls herself a prophetess and is teaching and seducing my servants to practice sexual immorality and to eat food sacrificed to idols. (Revelation 2:20)

ἀλλ' ἔχω κατὰ σοῦ ὅτι ἀφεῖς τὴν γυναῖκα Ἰεζάβελ, ἡ λέγουσα ἑαυτὴν προφῆτιν καὶ διδάσκει καὶ πλανᾷ τοὺς ἐμοὺς δούλους πορνεῦσαι καὶ φαγεῖν εἰδωλόθυτα. (ΑΠΟΚΑΛΥΨΙΣ ΙΩΑΝΝΟΥ 2:20)

The motto of the United States Centers for Disease Control and Prevention (CDC) is, "Saving Lives, Protecting People." Their mission is to "protect America from health, safety, and security threats" in the form of disease. One of the ways the CDC does this is through twenty quarantine stations around the USA. If ill persons attempt to enter the country, medical professionals examine them and decide whether they present a health hazard to citizens.

There are certain diseases against which the USA will take strict action, such as cholera, plague, viral hemorrhagic fevers, and yellow fever. If travelers are found to have these, the medical staff is likely to quarantine them until they recover. If the CDC didn't act, thousands or millions of citizens could become ill or die.

In Revelation 2:20, an outbreak of sinful living, caused by a woman termed "Jezebel," had begun to occur among the holy believers in Thyatira. Calling herself a prophetess, this woman was teaching the Christians that it was okay for them to participate in their guilds' pagan festivals. Thus, God's saints were practicing sexual immorality and idolatry. Jesus doesn't give the false prophetess's real name. Instead, He calls her *"that woman Jezebel"* because her actions are reminiscent of the Jezebel we find in 1 Kings 16:29–31. That wicked Jezebel influenced her husband, Israel's King Ahab, to worship Baal. An enemy to God's people, she attempted to carry the Northern Kingdom of Israel into idol worship and immorality. (See 2 Kings 9:22.)

> *Jezebel* is a Hebrew name that means "where is the prince?" This was a ritualistic saying spoken during worship to Baal. The nuance behind the expression suggests "Baal is prince." The name was heavily associated with idolatry and wickedness. Hence it is a fitting for the Jezebel herself and the false prophetess in Thyatira.

SATAN AT WORK THROUGH JEZEBEL

Jesus uses a strong term in the Greek when He says Jezebel was "seducing" (*plana*) the Thyatrian believers. It means "to lead astray; to take off track." A form of the same word, "seducer" (*planon*), is used as a title for Satan in Revelation 12:9. Satan was working in the Thyatrian church through Jezebel. It sounds strong and it is. But Jesus is sending a clear warning that the devil doesn't come into our communities, churches, and homes with red horns and a pitchfork. He shows up in the form of people who tell us things that soothe our conscience and relax our standards.

When these individuals show up, they need to be quarantined or they will spread lots of harm.

Unfortunately, the leadership in the Thyatrian church hadn't stopped her. They were the church that had an emphasis on love. It's possible they felt it might not be very loving to be confrontational. Or maybe they felt that it was *their* job to love and *God's* job to judge. Have you ever heard this idea before? But Jesus responds and tells them He is upset with them because they "tolerate" her.

The word "tolerate" (*apheis*) in the Greek literally means "to forgive." It is found in a manner that means they kept on forgiving her, likely making excuses why they should keep on accepting her.[32] The problem is, Jezebel didn't want forgiveness. (See verse 21.) She didn't think she was wrong and refused to change her mind about what she was teaching. She was a cancer, eating away at the purity of the church. God expected the church to quarantine her to preserve its holiness. But they hadn't. The epidemic had grown worse.

God has called all of us to walk in love. (See John 13:35.) This includes confronting those we love when they do wrong. (See Matthew 18:15–17.) This requires making good judgments out of love and truth. It's impossible never to judge and those who say Christians should *never* judge misinterpret God's Word. On the contrary, God is adamant that those who have authority must stop wrongdoing when wrongdoers put others at risk.

Do you have authority from God? Who are you responsible for? If you are a parent, you have authority over your children. If you're a pastor, you have responsibility for your flock. If you're a police officer, you have authority in your jurisdiction. If you're a college student, you are responsible for what happens in your dorm room. If you use social media, you determine what shows up on your timeline.

This week, use your authority to keep your jurisdiction free from evil. That doesn't mean becoming a self-righteous fundamentalist. But it does mean being firm that you won't tolerate anything that is displeasing to God. Don't be afraid to quarantine anything that will harm those you love. Being responsible *is* God's love.

PRAYER FOR THE WEEK

Dear Heavenly Father—
I thank You that walking in Your love means standing for the truth.
Today, I pray that You give me strength to lead and the boldness to
confront evil when it poses a threat to my life and those to whom I am
responsible in this life. Holy Spirit, give me Your wisdom to make righ-
teous judgments and help me to protect those who are mine from the
plans of the devil. In Jesus's name, amen!

ACTIVITY FOR THE WEEK

Make a list of the people you are responsible for. Is there anything that
is threatening their lives? If there is, write those things down next to their
name. Now, come up with a plan. What will you do to protect them from
the enemy's attack? When you have prayerfully decided, talk it over with
the person. Get into agreement and execute the plan.

SCRIPTURES FOR THE WEEK

Matthew 7:3–5	Romans 16:17
Matthew 18:15–20	1 Corinthians 5:1–8
Romans 12:9	1 Thessalonians 5:21–22

28

A BED THAT WILL MAKE YOU SICK

I gave her time to repent, but she refuses to repent of her sexual immorality. Behold, I will throw her onto a sickbed, and those who commit adultery with her I will throw into great tribulation, unless they repent of her works... (Revelation 2:21–22)

καὶ ἔδωκα αὐτῇ χρόνον ἵνα μετανοήσῃ, καὶ οὐ θέλει μετανοῆσαι ἐκ τῆς πορνείας αὐτῆς. ἰδοὺ βάλλω αὐτὴν εἰς κλίνην καὶ τοὺς μοιχεύοντας μετ᾽ αὐτῆς εἰς θλῖψιν μεγάλην, ἐὰν μὴ μετανοήσωσιν ἐκ τῶν ἔργων αὐτῆς...

(ΑΠΟΚΑΛΥΨΙΣ ΙΩΑΝΝΟΥ 2:21–22)

One million people around the world died from AIDS-related illnesses in 2016, according to hiv.gov. That's roughly the population of San

Jose, California. The government website also reports that as of July 2017, 36.7 million people worldwide were living with HIV or AIDS, which is nearly the population of the world's most crowded city, Tokyo, Japan.

Regarding other sexually transmitted diseases (STDs), the World Health Organization estimates that every year, there are 357 million new infections of the top four: chlamydia, gonorrhea, syphilis, and trichomoniasis. It's estimated that more than 500 million people have genital infection with herpes simplex virus. More than 290 million women have a human papillomavirus infection.

With these numbers, it's clear that promiscuity has created profound health problems for the world. But our mental, emotional, and spiritual health is also at stake.

In their book *Hooked*, Drs. Joe McIlhaney and Freda McKissic Bush discuss the profound bonding that takes place between two people when sexual intimacy occurs[33]: "When two people join physically, powerful neurohormones are released because of the sexual experience, making an impression on the brain and on the synapses in their brains and hardwiring their bond." The two doctors go on to explain that when this bond is broken, "the neurochemical imprint of that sexual experience remains, often for many years, impeding the very bonding process that leads to future healthy relationships."

The statistics in *Hooked* are shocking:

+ Young people who have had premarital sex are three times more likely to be depressed than their virgin friends.

+ Girls who have had sex are three times more likely to attempt suicide and boys are seven times more likely.

+ Those who are not virgins when they marry are more likely to divorce than those who marry as virgins.

+ Monogamous married couples report more sexual satisfaction than unmarried persons with multiple partners.

While these statistics might be new to us, God's Word has told us from the start that sexual sin is one of the reasons for a myriad of the world's issues. Nobody knew this better than the Thyatrian church.

Jezebel had brought sexual promiscuity into the church. God warned her it was going to harm her and the others who had gotten involved. Jesus says He "gave" (edōka) her time to repent. "Gave" (edōka), in this usage, emphasizes the fact that there was a definite time when Jesus extended mercy to Jezebel for her sexual sin so she could avoid any trouble her sin might earn.[34] Jesus always gives people a chance because He is loving and slow to anger. (See Psalm 103:8.) This should be an encouragement to you, especially if you've recently made a mistake. God wants you to turn back to Him and move forward, and He provides us with His grace and mercy to do it.

JEZEBEL REFUSED GOD'S MERCY

Yet, Jezebel didn't want God's mercy. Jesus said, "She refuses" (ou thelei). The Greek literally says "wishes not" for it. It is found in a tense that emphasizes: 1) she wished not to repent the first time she was given the opportunity; 2) she continued to keep on refusing God's mercy; and 3) she wasn't going to stop.[35] Perhaps she felt that if punishment didn't come right away, it was probably never going to come, so why stop? People think like that today, too. They think if there aren't immediate consequences, they've gotten away with something. Not quite. God's being patient. He gives us time to receive His mercy and change before bigger problems come. And they will come. (See John 16:33.)

In ancient Greek, klinē had also been used to describe a bier, the frame that a coffin is placed on before burial. There's no doubt that negative connotations surrounded this word. Hearing Jesus mention it would concern the believers in Thyatira.

Needless to say, Jezebel's time for mercy had expired. Jesus said He would have to "throw her onto a sickbed." This is an interesting expression. The word "throw" (ballō) here means to drag from one place to another. Sickbed (klinē) referred to a stretcher where sick people were laid. Jezebel's persistence in sexual sin was about to cause her to experience a debilitating sickness. Jesus was going to end up dragging her from the sensual bed of her fornication onto a stretcher. She refused to heed God's warning and now she was going to have to experience the kind of misery sexual sin brings—whatever form it took. God's Word here is painting a vivid picture for us. Sex outside of God's intent starts off exciting, but ends in pain.

Sex was God's idea. He created it for humans to create life and enjoy. When we go outside of God's design for sex, it destroys life and causes anguish. God never meant for sex to put us in a hospital, a psychiatric ward, or a counseling office. He meant for it to be one of our favorite things to enjoy—something that recharges us and gives us strength. But we need to do it His way, within the bounds of marriage.

In this day and age, when sex is constantly fed into our social media streams, we need to remind ourselves that promiscuity will end up putting us on a stretcher. If you've made a mistake (or mistakes), God's mercy has you reading this. It's not too late to change your behavior and avoid the sickbed. This week, don't believe the lies the world says about sex. The facts don't lie and neither does God's Word. The way God meant sex to be will always be healthier…and better.

PRAYER FOR THE WEEK

Dear Heavenly Father—
I thank You that You have created sex for me to enjoy. It is Your idea and it is intended to give me a healthy and wonderful life. But I realize I must do things within Your order. Father, I commit my sexual life to you. I resolve today to keep sex within the bounds of marriage, reserving sex only for my marriage. I declare that my life will be full of physical strength and emotional peace as a result. In Jesus's name, amen!

ACTIVITY FOR THE WEEK

Break off any unhealthy sexual relationships. Delete numbers in your phone and unfriend people on social media who contribute toward any sexual impurity in your life.

SCRIPTURES FOR THE WEEK

Genesis 2:23–25

Proverbs 5:18–19

1 Corinthians 6:18–20

1 Corinthians 7:1–2

1 Thessalonians 4:3–5

Hebrews 13:4

29

THRIFT STORE
SPIRITUALITY

But to the rest of you in Thyatira, who do not hold this teaching, who have not learned what some call the deep things of Satan, to you I say, I do not lay on you any other burden.

(Revelation 2:24)

ὑμῖν δὲ λέγω τοῖς λοιποῖς τοῖς ἐν Θυατείροις, ὅσοι οὐκ ἔχουσιν τὴν διδαχὴν ταύτην, οἵτινες οὐκ ἔγνωσαν τὰ βαθέα τοῦ Σατανᾶ ὡς λέγουσιν· οὐ βάλλω ἐφ᾽ ὑμᾶς ἄλλο βάρος. (ΑΠΟΚΑΛΥΨΙΣ ΙΩΑΝΝΟΥ 2:24)

Live a little and you'll realize you need a philosophy. You know, a way of making sense of this life and dealing with all the malarkey. Unless you're just a flat-out atheist, your philosophy includes some form of spirituality in the traditional sense of the word. We all get our spirituality from somewhere and I've noticed that social media is sort of the thrift store, if you will.

The thrift store has no particular sort of style. It's not like going to Macy's, Kohl's, or Target. When you leave the thrift store, you could end up wearing Doc Martens from 1998, acid-washed jeans from 1986, and some red and white T-shirt from an unknown era that reads, "I gave blood to the Red Cross." Random, but it fits you...for now.

Today on social media, all sorts of random quotes fly around that people adopt for their life because it fits them...for now. But since there is no reasoning behind *why* the quote was said, people can easily remove it from their life the moment it goes out of style or no longer fits their agenda.

Here are a few quotes I just pulled off of social media:

"Just be."

"Actually, I can."

"Self-love is the greatest medicine."

"Just because my path is different doesn't mean I'm lost."

"You are imperfect permanently and inevitably flawed. And you are beautiful."

I promise I didn't work hard to find these for the sake of making a point; they popped right up—and I could add 10,000 more. Notice a few things about these quotes? They are all about *me, me, me* and enjoying who *I am* without ever having to change, because having to change is *so* offensive.

God's Word doesn't say any of this. In fact, it says the opposite.[36] Right now, people everywhere, including Christians, are bebopping around for expressions of spirituality to add to their philosophy on life. The sad thing is, if they are expressions like the ones above, they're not a good look.

Some of the believers in Thyatira had been shopping around for new expressions of spirituality. Jezebel took advantage of this. She taught them that they would appreciate the grace of God more if they indulged more in their sinful desires. This led them into sexual sin, idolatry, and a knowledge of the occult. Their spirituality looked like a wacky outfit from the thrift store and just didn't match. Nevertheless, their pride swelled. They began to refer to their philosophy as "the deep things of God."

BEWARE CUTE FUZZIES FROM SATAN

Have you ever met someone who has taken grace out of proportion in order to indulge their immoral lifestyle and considered themselves more spiritual for it? They think God accepts their lifestyle and this magnifies the depth of His love. Makes a pretty little Instagram quote. Might feel soft and fuzzy, too. Be careful not to adapt it though; Jesus modifies the statement and calls this *the deep things of Satan*!

The word "Satan" (*Satana*) here is being used to specify "source."[37] It means that despite the cute, cozy nature this form of spirituality appeared to have, it came from Satan. The deceiver is the source of sweet-sounding, attractive-looking forms of spirituality that make us feel better about ourselves. We must be careful not to pick them up, lest we put them on.

> The Greek word *Satana* is borrowed from the Hebrew/Aramaic word śātān, which means "one lying in ambush for." When we hear this name, we are given the vivid picture of an adversary who watches us and plots our demise.

God wants your philosophy and outlook on life to grow in the deep things of Him. For this to be possible, you can't depend on sorting through other people's stuff on social media. Instead, you'll have to put your nose in God's Word and study it regularly, allowing the truly deep things to unfold to you. When they do, you'll see that true spirituality draws us closer to God and further from sin. That's grace and it's the best philosophy in life to have.

PRAYER FOR THE WEEK

Dear Heavenly Father—
I thank You that You desire me to abide in Your Word and know the truth, as you promise in John 8:31–32. It is my desire to develop a profound spirituality from Your holy Word. Holy Spirit, give to me wisdom and revelation as I study Your Word. Protect my heart from

things that sound good but have their source in the devil and take me further from the truth. In Jesus's name, Amen

ACTIVITY FOR THE WEEK

Find five to ten "positive" quotes floating around social media, not including those from Scripture. Analyze them. Are they truly what God's Word says? Do they promote the power of Christ and His Holy Spirit in us? Or do they suggest our inherent good apart from God? How could embracing these affect your philosophy and, ultimately, your walk with the Lord?

SCRIPTURES FOR THE WEEK

Joshua 1:8

Psalm 119:15–16

Proverbs 3:1–2

Acts 17:11

2 Timothy 2:15

2 Timothy 3:14–15

30

PUT TOGETHER A SPIRITUAL WINNING STREAK

The one who conquers and who keeps my works until the end, to him I will give authority over the nations, and he will rule them with a rod of iron, as when earthen pots are broken in pieces, even as I myself have received authority from my Father. (Revelation 2:26–27)

καὶ ὁ νικῶν καὶ ὁ τηρῶν ἄχρι τέλους τὰ ἔργα μου, δώσω αὐτῷ ἐξουσίαν ἐπὶ τῶν ἐθνῶν καὶ ποιμανεῖ αὐτοὺς ἐν ῥάβδῳ σιδηρᾷ ὡς τὰ σκεύη τὰ κεραμικὰ συντρίβεται, ὡς κἀγὼ εἴληφα παρὰ τοῦ πατρός μου.

(ΑΠΟΚΑΛΥΨΙΣ ΙΩΑΝΝΟΥ 2:26–27)

I've often considered attempting to become a contestant on *Jeopardy!*[38] I *am* a trivia buff and I'm pretty sure I know a little about a lot. I also imagine I have a quick buzzer finger. If I got on the show, I'd like to believe I could do some damage. But no matter how well I might fare, I'd need a miracle from heaven for a winning streak like *Jeopardy!*'s most acclaimed contestant, Ken Jennings. Even you've never caught an episode of this quiz show (which I think is impossible if you live in the USA and own a television), it's likely you remember who he is.

On June 2, 2004, Jennings played his first round and barely pulled out a victory. Yet, he went on to win seventy-four consecutive games and amassed $2,520,700 in total winnings during his time. Perhaps the most impressive statistic of all is that in 87 percent of his games, he stockpiled more than twice as much money as the opponent closest to him, safeguarding his win before entering Final Jeopardy. He was dominant. Jennings' run is the height of a win streak. People love win streaks because they create momentum and momentum brings victory.

Take it from Jerry Seinfeld, maybe the most successful stand-up comic of our time. Seinfeld once shared a secret to success with another young comic. He explained that to be a better comedian, he needed to have better jokes. In order to have better jokes, he needed to write every day. Once, to motivate himself to write jokes, Seinfeld hung up a big wall calendar and put a red "X" over each day he wrote. He worked hard to keep his chain of "X's" from breaking. Jerry told the young comic, "After a few days, you'll have a chain…You'll like seeing that chain, especially when you get a few weeks under your belt." Win streak. Momentum. Victory.

In Revelation 2:26–27, Jesus teaches the church in Thyatira that building a win streak over sin would equate to tremendous victory in their walk with God. This is seen when He says the reward for conquering sin is *"authority over the nations"* and that, as a result, they *"will rule them* [the nations] *with a rod of iron."* In the most immediate context, Jesus is telling the conquering church that they will join with Him in His future rule over the nations of earth. (See Revelation 19:15.) But there is also a principle in this that we shouldn't miss: authority comes from conquering.

JESUS: EXERCISE AUTHORITY OVER SIN

The Greek word for "authority" (*exousia*) means "the ability to perform an action; control over something; capability." For example, you could say a NASCAR driver has authority over the track. They drive in a commanding manner and are capable of handling the turns with ease. This comes from conquering the turns over and over again. Each success becomes part of a streak of successes, adding to the driver's capabilities and command. In much the same way, conquering *temptations to sin* will build the momentum you have over *sin* and make it all the easier for you to drive over it.

> Shepherds defended their flock with a hard crook, often made of oak, that had a knob at the end. Sometimes, the knob had nails and sharp objects driven into it for further protection. It's believed that kingly scepters derived from the shepherd's crook, as kings were the shepherds of their people.

When you've gained authority, you're in a position to "rule" (*poimēn*). This word here means "to shepherd." We often think of shepherds as being nice and tender. But shepherds were also tough cookies. They had to kill wild animals and destroy vicious predators. They had the rule over their flocks and if anything compromised that, they smashed it over the head with their crook.

Are you smashing temptation over the head these days? Is it tough to resist screenshotting gossip and sending it to your friends? Are you resisting opportunities to disrespect your spouse? If you can't answer yes, you aren't ruling yet. You need some wins and you need some momentum.

Let me give you a personal testimony: at the time of this writing, I'm unmarried and past thirty. But believe it or not, I'm still a virgin. I've been able to successfully guard my purity until I give it to my future wife. One of the main reasons I've had authority in this area of my life and have been able to rule over sexual sin is because each day has been a win. And the more I've won, the easier it's become. If I had let myself take a loss early on, it's more than likely I'd have plenty more by now. But the victories in God have given me authority in God, which has given me the ability to keep smashing sin in its head.

This week, it's time to get a streak going. How about expecting to go the whole week without messing up? When the first temptation comes creeping your way, smash its head really hard. It will likely be easier the next time. You are building up that momentum and you are ruling with authority. Isn't that a whole lot better than losing?

PRAYER FOR THE WEEK

Dear Heavenly Father—
It is Your desire for me to win, to walk in authority, and to rule over temptation and sin. Help me, Holy Spirit, to put some consecutive wins on the board this week. I pray for momentum in holiness. I declare nothing the enemy brings my way this week shall slow that momentum. Instead, I will roll over the works of the devil with great power. In Jesus's name, amen!

ACTIVITY FOR THE WEEK

Create a calendar. Either hang one on your wall or use your computer or phone; it should be someplace where you will see it frequently. Put a red "X" or a specific mark on each day you are victorious over temptation. Keep that chain going! Ask the Holy Spirit for His help each morning and be sure to fill your heart with God's Word all day. (See Psalm 119:11.) At the end of the week, evaluate how it went. Do you have more momentum going into the new week?

SCRIPTURES FOR THE WEEK

Romans 2:7	1 Thessalonians 3:13
1 Corinthians 15:58	1 Thessalonians 4:1
Galatians 6:9	2 Thessalonians 3:13

31

"THE GLOW"

And I will give him the morning star. (Revelation 2:28)

καὶ δώσω αὐτῷ τὸν ἀστέρα τὸν πρωϊνόν.
(ΑΠΟΚΑΛΥΨΙΣ ΙΩΑΝΝΟΥ 2:28)

You either have "it" or you don't. Well, that's at least what they say in showbiz, I think. Showbiz is a tough business and hardly anyone makes it. If *you're* going to make it, there has to be that obscure something—known as "it" or "the X-factor"—that launches you there...plus a whole lot of luck, or blessing, or "pull," or whatever you want to call it. Television producers realized in the early 2000s that society was interested in watching people "make it." Along came *Pop Idol, American Idol, Arab Idol, Indonesian Idol, New Zealand Idol, The Voice, the X-Factor*—you get the point, right? Suddenly, the whole world gets to see, from their living room sofas, what "it" is and what "it" isn't.

In 2007, I'll admit, I got into "it." I was among the thirty million weekly viewers watching the contestants rise and fall on *American Idol Season 6*. I found the show fascinating because some of the better singers, I felt, were eliminated early and some of the more attractive talents didn't stick around long. This told me that "it" was beyond looks and talent. It seemed that those who did well had an indescribable magnetism that drew you to keep watching, even if you *didn't* like them. For example, there was a particular contestant my mother didn't like. She couldn't stand this person. I'd call her and all she'd talk about is how she hoped they were going to get eliminated soon. But my mom was always glued to the TV waiting for them to perform. And when they *did* get eliminated, she missed watching them! She missed "it," the "X-factor." It's compelling.

In Revelation 2:28, Jesus tells the church in Thyatira about the spiritual "it" factor. He makes another promise to those who overcome sin and tells them He will give them *"the morning star"* (*ton astera ton prōinon*). In Greco-Roman times, this term was an idiom for the planet Venus because in the morning, it shines brilliantly. It symbolized power and royalty. In its most immediate context, when Jesus says He is going to give us the morning star, He is promising us that we will share in His Messianic reign over the earth when He returns. (See Numbers 24:17; Daniel 12:3.)

WE CAN REFLECT GOD'S GLORY

But, for the present, there is a mission for each of us: until Jesus comes, we can reflect His glory to the darkness that surrounds if we live in close proximity to Him. We won't call this "it." We'll call it "the glow," the splendor of countenance that comes from living holy and being in the presence of God.

Venus was the Roman goddess of love ("Aphrodite" in the Greek). The Romans named the brightest object in the sky (besides the sun and moon) after her. The Greeks thought Venus was two different celestial bodies and called them "the Morning Star" and "the Evening Star."

Think of the planet Venus. It is the brightest planet in our sky. But Venus has no light of its own. If the sun stopped shining, it would be lights out for Venus. Venus's light is just a reflection of the sun's. And as long Venus maintains its close proximity to the sun, it will continue to reflect the sun's glory.

Human beings were created by God to live in close proximity to Him so we can reflect His glory and splendor. As a result, each of us *can* and should *have* "the glow." Take Stephen, for example. (See Acts 6:5.) He was full of the Holy Spirit and before the darkest moment of his life, facing certain death, his face radiated like an angel's. (See Acts 6:15.) Without a relationship with the Lord, I'm certain Stephen's expression would have been abysmal and tormented. But he was so close to God, bad times couldn't keep God's light from reflecting upon his face. Circumstances don't determine whether or not we shine. Our proximity to God does.

Jesus warned the church in Thyatira about sin because sin distances us from God and causes "the glow" to become dimmer. When you see people with misery and torment on their faces, you are seeing people who are lost in the universe, too far from the sun to reflect it.

For example, there was a rapper who was killed during the writing of this book. Social media was in an uproar. I hadn't heard of him, so I checked out some of his social pages. My heart broke when I saw the darkness on his face and the rage in his eyes. I wasn't surprised that his lyrics were violent and his death was reminiscent of the things he had sung about. It's apparent he had deep inner struggles, but his biggest problem was that he had no proximity to God. This young man had charisma, "it," the X-factor—if only he had found Jesus, he could have also had "the glow." The outcome of his life would have been different and he could have helped his millions of fans find *true* joy and peace.

While the world seeks after "it," spend your time seeking after "the glow." Don't waste your life coveting personal magnetism that draws fans or Facebook "likes." That fades. Rather, desire the brilliant countenance that comes from living holy and being in the presence of God. This will give you eternal influence and, trust me, people are less likely to forget you. Nobody forgets the eyes of Jesus, even when they're peeking through yours.

PRAYER FOR THE WEEK

Dear Heavenly Father—
I thank You that I am a reflector of Your glory and splendor. I pray
that I will live in close proximity of Your presence this week so that I
may shine Your light for all to see. When people see me, may they see
Jesus Christ who lives within. When they look into my eyes, may they
sense the love, compassion, and boldness of the Lord peeking at them.
May my countenance be a witness for the world in darkness to see. And
may many people see Your light in me and turn from the darkness. In
Jesus's name, amen!

ACTIVITY FOR THE WEEK

Go stargazing! Try to find the planet Venus in the morning or night
sky. When you are peering at it, journal. How does Venus contrast with
the rest of the sky? Does your life stand out the way Venus does?

SCRIPTURES FOR THE WEEK

Job 11:17	Proverbs 13:9
Psalm 97:11	Daniel 12:3
Proverbs 4:18	Matthew 5:14–16

PART VI

THE CHURCH AT SARDIS— STUDIES ON THE HOLY SPIRIT

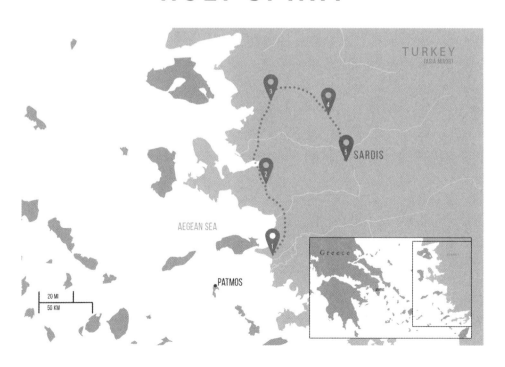

32

WHAT GOOD IS *JUST* A NAME?

And to the angel of the church in Sardis write: The words of him who has the seven spirits of God and the seven stars. I know your works. You have the reputation of being alive, but you are dead. (Revelation 3:1)

Καὶ τῷ ἀγγέλῳ τῆς ἐν Σάρδεσιν ἐκκλησίας γράψον Τάδε λέγει ὁ ἔχων τὰ ἑπτὰ πνεύματα τοῦ θεοῦ καὶ τοὺς ἑπτὰ ἀστέρας Οἶδά σου τὰ ἔργα ὅτι ὄνομα ἔχεις ὅτι ζῆς, καὶ νεκρὸς εἶ. (ΑΠΟΚΑΛΥΨΙΣ ΙΩΑΝΝΟΥ 3:1)

Friday nights don't live up to their name. We say "TGIF" like were going to do something awesome and crazy, but the majority of us end up under the blanket, catching up on memes, and binging on *Fuller House*.

(Well, maybe not.) You likely order Papa John's instead of cooking—*real* crazy of you. (I hope you sense my sarcasm.) When I was twenty-one, I gave up on Friday nights. I always *felt* like I needed to do something amazing because it was *Friday*. I'd spend most of my night trying to figure out *what* to do until it got too late to do anything at all. And for that reason, I don't like Friday nights—all hype, no delivery. I prefer Thursday nights, even Tuesday nights, over Friday nights. I just can't stand the hysteria. It has a name and nothing to back it. (And if I've misjudged and *your* Friday nights happen to be Ah-*May*-Zing!…more power to ya. Please tell the other 99.7 percent of us what we're doing wrong.)

The church in Sardis, like a Friday night, had a big name but nothing behind it. It *appeared* that they had it going on, but Jesus said they were on life support and about to die. While they didn't face persecution, the Sardian believers were worse off than the other churches. The lack of persecution wasn't exactly a plus—there was no persecution because the church was so comatose, it wasn't worth attacking. Jesus gives them the most severe admonishment of the seven churches and diagnoses their problem, saying: *"You have the reputation of being alive, but you are dead."*

This Sardian church had a great reputation. The Greek confirms this: "reputation" (*onoma*) means "fame; well-known." The verb, "have" (*echeis*), is in a tense that stresses ongoing and continuous action.[39] This means that the Sardian church had ongoing fame that continued to spread around the region. It's imaginable that all over Asia Minor, people would have said, "Oh, yes, the church at Sardis; aren't they something! Man, their last conference was on fire!" Other pastors probably envied the Sardian church and wished they could lead it. It's likely that if Sardis had an Instagram account, their posts would be a mix of cutting-edge design work and sharp quotes, with more than three thousand comments, being mostly the fire emoji and users tagging their friends: "Hey @aeschylus4568, check this out girl!"

> The synagogue of Sardis was one of the largest of the ancient world. It was a magnificent structure, with mosaic floors and plenty of marble. It attests to the vitality of Jewish communities in Asia Minor and the splendor of Sardis.

CITY DIED...AND SO DID THE CHURCH

Yet, Jesus told them that they weren't as alive as they appeared. He goes so far as to say, *"But you are dead."* He uses *kai* for "but" instead of the usual *alla*, because *kai* is stronger and draws a sharper comparison.[40] *Kai* adds a strong tone of dissent and beefs up Christ's sense of objection. While everyone was thinking the Sardian church was so full of spiritual life, Jesus was saying with very strong disagreement that it was lifeless. According to Jesus, the Sardian church couldn't be more opposite to what the other churches thought. It was rotting from apathy, Christians in name only.

There's an interesting parallel between the Sardian church and the city of Sardis itself. When Sardis was founded, seven centuries before the letter to the Sardians, it was one of the most splendid cities in all the world. It was ruled by King Croesus, who had helped it attain incredible wealth. Yet, when this letter was written, the city of Sardis had deteriorated. Ancient monuments stood around the city, reminders of what used to be...and was no longer. The city had died and all it had left was its name—but what good is *just* a name? Christ didn't like to see His church die the same way.

Remember, this week, that a healthy spiritual life is not determined by what others say about you. Their names mean nothing. They never know the full story and that's why their admiration should never go to your head. Our spiritual well-being is dependent only on what Jesus says because He knows it all. So, forget the comments, the emojis, the likes, and the shares. Be wise and focus on the name you have with Jesus. He's the one who knows whether you are alive or dead.

PRAYER FOR THE WEEK

Dear Heavenly Father—
I don't want an empty reputation that isn't backed by Your integrity and power, and I never want to be a Christian in name only. I want my actions to line up with the things I say and proclaim. Never let me fall back into apathy; rather, keep the flame of Your Holy Spirit burning inside of me so that my spiritual life will always be full of life. In Jesus' name, amen!

ACTIVITY FOR THE WEEK

Draw your name in the middle of a piece of paper. Place a circle around it and create a mind map. From out of your name, connect words and things that God might say about your personal life right now. Ask the Holy Spirit to search your heart. As He does, be sure to include the good and bad. When you are done, look at the paper. Is this what you want your name to be before God? If it is, praise God! If it isn't, pray over it and ask the Holy Spirit to help you change.

SCRIPTURES FOR THE WEEK

Isaiah 12:42–43	Matthew 15:8–9
Ezekiel 33:31	John 5:44
Amos 5:21–24	John 12:42–43

33

THE SPIRIT REVIVES

And to the angel of the church in Sardis write: The words of him who has the seven spirits of God and the seven stars. I know your works. You have the reputation of being alive, but you are dead. (Revelation 3:1)

Καὶ τῷ ἀγγέλῳ τῆς ἐν Σάρδεσιν ἐκκλησίας γράψον Τάδε λέγει ὁ ἔχων τὰ ἑπτὰ πνεύματα τοῦ θεοῦ καὶ τοὺς ἑπτὰ ἀστέρας Οἶδά σου τὰ ἔργα ὅτι ὄνομα ἔχεις ὅτι ζῇς, καὶ νεκρὸς εἶ. (ΑΠΟΚΑΛΥΨΙΣ ΙΩΑΝΝΟΥ 3:1)

Midwest winters are chilling, especially in the north, where hats and gloves are musts. Staying outside for long periods is not an option. That's why Paulie Hynek, a two-year-old from Eau Claire, Wisconsin, stepped into danger when he wandered out of his parents' farm house one black, winter night in 2001. CBS Minnesota reported the story in 2011, ten years after it happened.

When Paulie's parents woke up, they realized he was missing. Frantically, they began searching for him until they found him lying in a snowbank. It was two degrees below zero. Paulie's body temperature had plummeted from the average healthy temperature of 98.6, to just 60. (The body shuts down somewhere around 70.) Paulie was dead. Aghast, Paulie's mom called 911 and told the operator that she had lost her son. However, the operator, gave her a reason to hope and told her there might be something that they could do.

A Mayo Clinic helicopter was dispatched and flew Paulie to the hospital in Eau Claire. He didn't show any signs of life: no heartbeat, no breathing, not even any brain activity. But the doctors didn't give up. They believed that if they could warm him up, they might be able to get Paulie back to life. So, they began by giving him a warm IV and then started circulating his blood using a machine. Sure enough, it worked. Paulie's heartbeat started again and he came back to life. When talking to reporters, Dr. Robert Weichmann said the event was miraculous. "There had to be some wonderful spirit inside this boy."

Whether the doctor realized it or not, he was making a profound statement. He identified a connection between life and spirit. God's Word makes a similar statement, only not in reference to the human spirit, but to God's Spirit. *"It is the Spirit who gives life"* (John 6:63). The presence of the Holy Spirit is the source of our spiritual life and vitality. Without His Spirit, our spiritual lives will grow cold and die, like the Sardian Church. They were missing the presence of the Holy Spirit, and they were waning and dying. But Jesus assured them that His Spirit could revive them back to life. And He communicated this by revealing Himself to them as *"him who has the seven spirits of God and the seven stars."*

The seven spirits of God represent seven functions of the Holy Spirit that make up His fullness. (See Isaiah 11:2–4.) Referring to the seven spirits is just a way of saying the fullness of the power of the Holy Spirit.

Aside from the Greek articles (like "the" and "a" in English), *kai* ("and") is the most used Greek word in the New Testament. It occurs 9,153 times.

The Greek word "and" (*kai*) tells us something additional and important. It is being used to clarify and explain the seven spirits of God.[41] This means that the seven spirits of God *are* the seven stars. When Jesus says the seven spirits *are* the seven stars (the seven churches; see chapter two), he simply means that the presence and ministry of the Holy Spirit is found living within the church.

If you've ever watched a Big 10 college football game, you've probably heard the raucous cheer from Nittany Lions fans, "We *are*—Penn State!" What they mean is, they are the university and it wouldn't be anything without its people. It's the same with the Holy Spirit: He makes churches what they are. Think about it. Who is responsible for all the healings? Who anoints the pastor to preach? Where do prophecies and words of knowledge come from? The Spirit of God.

JESUS HAS THE POWER OF THE SPIRIT

Jesus tells the Sardians that He "has" (*echōn*) the seven spirits; it was at His disposal to give. Jesus is the one who sends the power of the Spirit into our churches and personal lives. (See Matthew 3:11; Luke 24:49.) This would have encouraged the Sardians and given them hope. Though they were dying, if they repented and asked the Lord to be revived, He was willing and able to put His Spirit back into their midst. Jesus didn't want to see them die; He wanted them to have a revival of His Holy Spirit. He wanted to start their hearts back up and get them on their feet and going with the power of the Spirit and the fullness of His gifts.

It's possible that you may need a revival in your spiritual life right now. Perhaps you've grown cold and the pulse of your zeal has slowed down. Has it been a long time since the gifts of the Holy Spirit have operated through you? Perhaps you had been used by God to prophecy, speak in tongues, or cast out devils, but haven't functioned in that way in a long time because you've grown apathetic. Jesus is inviting you now to receive a revival of His Spirit. If you will only seek Him this week, He can give you a fresh outpouring of His Holy Spirit and revive everything dying in your life. Will you let Him have your heart so He can place His Spirit inside?

PRAYER FOR THE WEEK

Dear Heavenly Father—
More than anything, I want the fullness of the power of Your Holy
Spirit in my life. I want the full measure of His gift and graces. Stir
inside of me a desire to be revived by the Spirit. Revive my prayer life,
revive my zeal, revive every gift that I once walked in. Lord Jesus, touch
me right now. May every dead thing come back to life and may I be
filled with Your Spirit to overflowing. In Jesus's name, amen!

ACTIVITY FOR THE WEEK

Fast and pray. Give up a meal a day (or more) to seek the face of God
for a fresh outpouring of His Spirit. Specifically, ask God for a fresh filling
(see Acts 4:31) and for evidence and manifestation of that fresh filling in
your life.

SCRIPTURES FOR THE WEEK

Ezekiel 11:19	Acts 2:1–4
Ezekiel 36:26–27	Romans 8:14–17
Acts 1:8	Galatians 4:6

34

HOW TO STAY ON TOP

*Wake up, and strengthen what remains and is about to die, for
I have not found your works complete in the sight of my God.*
(Revelation 3:2)

γίνου γρηγορῶν καὶ στήρισον τὰ λοιπὰ ἃ ἔμελλον ἀποθα-
νεῖν, οὐ γὰρ εὕρηκά σου τὰ ἔργα πεπληρωμένα ἐνώπιον
τοῦ θεοῦ μου. (ΑΠΟΚΑΛΥΨΙΣ ΙΩΑΝΝΟΥ 3:2)

The Golden State Warriors blew a 3-1 lead in the NBA Finals. Recognize
this? If you do, you know your memes. If not, allow me to enlighten.
In 2016, the Golden State Warriors of Oakland, California, were on their
way to winning the NBA finals and becoming back-to-back champions.
They had taken a commanding lead, three games to one, in a best-of-sev-
en series against their opponent, the Cavaliers of Cleveland, Ohio, led by
Lebron James. Twitterverse was going nuts, having all sorts of fun trolling
James and the Cavs. No team had ever come back in the NBA finals to win

after falling behind 3-1. It was unimaginable...unthinkable...impossible. The Warriors and their fans had the champagne on ice. That's when the Cavs mounted their offensive attack.

Cleveland's Lebron James and Kyrie Irving became unstoppable. In game five, both players scored 41 points. Each. Their assault didn't stop in game six: James scored another 41 points and Irving handily scored 23. The Warriors were stunned and their spirits were starting to flatten. And the swelling Cavs didn't stop in game seven: their 93 points were enough to shove the reigning champs off the throne to become the new kings of the NBA. The trolls on social media had a field day for, literally, over a year. Somehow, the straightforward and grammatically precise phrase *The Golden State Warriors blew a 3-1 lead in the NBA Finals* went viral. People were posting it everywhere and under everything. It would show up under the president's posts, under celebrity posts, under church posts—you name it. It emasculated the Warriors and served as a reminder that getting too chill can cost you your spirit.

The church at Sardis had become too chill. In spiritual terms, this is called being apathetic. They were about to blow more than a 3-1 lead; they were about to blow their relationship with God. A deep spiritual sleep had come over them, making them passive toward the sinful culture. No longer did they have an urgency to testify and affect the pagan world for Jesus. They had gotten lazy, complacent, and content.

There's another interesting parallel between the Sardian church and the city of Sardis here. During the sixth century B.C., when the citadel of Sardis was at the height of its power, its citizens didn't think it could ever be overtaken. When Sardis' King Croesus went to war with Persia's King Cyrus, Croesus was positive he was safe behind Sardis' walls, untroubled about the Persians, because he didn't think they could scale the citadel. So, he left it completely unguarded. Cyrus's men eventually found a way up. When they got to the top, the Sardians weren't prepared to fight and the city fell into Persian hands.

Ancient Greeks attributed the invention of the lyre to the god Hermes. Lyre players often wore long gowns as costumes and accompanied their music with poetry and singing. The ancient lyre stands as a symbol for musical arts.

After Cyrus conquered the city, he wanted to make sure it never rebelled, so he forbade the Sardians from having weapons. He also enforced a law that men had to teach their sons lyre-playing, dance, and trade. This emasculated the men. Their spirits had been taken from them. The city continued like this for years to come while under Persian rule.

JESUS: GO TO RED ALERT

It's likely every Sardian in the Sardis church knew this story. That's why Jesus tells them, *Wake up!*" (*ginou grēgorōn*). The word "wake up" (*gregoreo*) means "to be watchful; to be in constant readiness; to be on alert." It was used by Jesus in Matthew 24:43 to describe how a person would act if they knew a thief was going to break into their house. It is found in a manner that means attentive, unwinking watching that doesn't end,[42] like a wide-eyed kid starring out the window during his first plane ride. Jesus is commanding the Sardians to continue to *watch*, *watch*, and keep on *watching*! In other words, the Sardians needed to stop being apathetic like King Croesus. They needed to care more about their spiritual lives; otherwise the presence of the Spirit would be taken from them. But God didn't want that. He wanted to remain with His people. That's why he tells them to "wake up" and "watch!"

The Holy Spirit moves among His people when they are paying attention to their spiritual lives. The moment we lose our consideration for the Holy Spirit and His place in our lives is the moment our spiritual victory starts to wane. To prevent this, we need to always be giving our spiritual disciplines—prayer, giving, worship, reading God's Word, etc.—time and attention. That's the surest way to stay on top.

Consider the person who used to come to church, all fired up and ready to worship. It's certain their lives were triumphant during those times. Then, they became too occupied and busy and, before you knew it, you never saw them again. You later find out that they now question what they once believed and their heart is hard. What happened? They became lax.

Missed a little church here, missed a little church there...then they fell asleep and blew a 3-1 lead.

God has carried you too far to get lax on Him now. Stay fervent, stay ready, and stay on top of your game. When you do this, you can be certain you won't lose the Spirit's wonderful presence. Your reign with Christ never has to come to an end.

PRAYER FOR THE WEEK

Dear Heavenly Father—
I thank You that I can always walk in Your Spirit and my reign with Christ never has to come to an end. As long as I stay on top of the disciplines that help me maintain my relationship with You, I can fully expect Your glory and presence in my life. But, Lord, I need Your grace to do so. Empower me with Your spirit to pray, to stay hungry so I can seek Your face, and to give me illumination and revelation from Your Word. As a result, I will stay secure in You. In Jesus's name, amen!

ACTIVITY FOR THE WEEK

Write out your game plan. What are the spiritual disciplines that keep you locked into the presence of God? Some of them should be going to church regularly, praying in the Spirit, meditating God's Word daily, and fasting. How often are you committed to doing these? What do you gain from each?

SCRIPTURES FOR THE WEEK

Acts 18:25	1 Corinthians 12:31
Acts 20:18–20	Colossians 4:12–13
Romans 12:11	2 Timothy 1:6–7

35

REBUILD WITH WHAT YOU HAVE

Wake up, and strengthen what remains and is about to die, for I have not found your works complete in the sight of my God.
(Revelation 3:2)

γίνου γρηγορῶν καὶ στήρισον τὰ λοιπὰ ἃ ἔμελλον ἀποθα-
νεῖν, οὐ γὰρ εὕρηκά σου τὰ ἔργα πεπληρωμένα ἐνώπιον
τοῦ θεοῦ μου.   (ΑΠΟΚΑΛΥΨΙΣ ΙΩΑΝΝΟΥ 3:2)

It took only one minute for 80 percent of San Francisco, California, to be demolished. The year was 1906. On Wednesday, April 18, at 5:12 a.m., a high-intensity 8.0 earthquake shook the Bay area and ripped up three hundred miles of the San Andreas Fault. The death toll reached 3,000 and

300,000 of the city's 410,000 citizens lost their homes. It remains one the worst natural disasters in the United States.

The most redeeming thing about this tragic occurrence is that San Francisco was speedily rebuilt. The city leaders got to work right away, using whatever means they had. Four days after the quake, three hundred plumbers were already repairing the water and sewage mains. In a few weeks, street cars were up and running. By April 30, train tracks were laid and rubble was being hauled off and dumped into Marina Bay. By June, banks were open and commerce resumed. During the summer, workers cut down redwood and Douglas firs to erect new buildings. Exactly a year after the quake, on April 18, 1907, the luxurious Fairmont Hotel opened. By 1909, the city had erected 20,000 new buildings. In 1915, San Francisco hosted a world's fair called the Panama Pacific Explosion to show off domes and colorful buildings that the city had erected in Marina Bay, on top of the old city. San Francisco was back, new and better than before. And it happened because the workers built using what they had.

You could say the church in Sardis was sort of like early twentieth-century San Francisco. Once alive and thriving, they found themselves in shambles. Jesus warned that they needed to start rebuilding their spiritual lives at once; otherwise they would die in the rubble. To do this, Jesus uses an interesting phrase. He says, *"strengthen what remains"* (*stērison ta loipa*). This statement is the key to spiritual renaissance and revival. If your spiritual life has been demolished, for whatever reason, following this statement is sure to make you a thriving believer once again.

> *Skêptron* is the Greek word for "cane" or "walking stick." The verbal form of this word, skeptomai, means "to lean" and "to support oneself." The English word "scepter" comes from *skêpton*.

"What remains" (*ta loipa*) refers to that which is left over. It could be used to describe crumbs from a loaf of bread that's been devoured or the population still alive after a devastating plague. Here, it refers to the virtues that survived their spiritual collapse. It refers to any grace or spiritual discipline they could work with and use to rebuild. Many times, even in our deepest crises where we feel distant from God, we may still maintain a weakened conviction about prayer or reading God's Word. We may still see some benefit in going to church or reaching out to another believer for help. That's at least something to work with. That's the place to start and that's where you begin rebuilding. But how?

REBUILD WITH WHAT YOU HAVE

Jesus tells us to strengthen those things. The Greek word for "strengthen" (*stērizo*) means to give support and commitment to something. It was used to describe people who walked with a cane. The cane lends constant care and support to a weak leg until, perhaps, it gets stronger. In the same way, giving constant care and support to those weakened virtues and disciplines that still exist in your life, despite your spiritual failure, will make them stronger. In turn, your relationship with God will get stronger and, eventually, every area of your spiritual life will be back up and running.

Let's use an example: let's say you are angry at God and you don't want to talk to Him and pray. Yet, you still enjoy listening to anointed worship. Bang—that's the place to start. Give constant attention to *that*. You will see when *that* gets stronger, other things will start getting stronger. You may want to start singing along with the music. That might turn into a true expression of worship for the first time in years. Before you know it, you are talking to your Father again. You may end up wanting to pray. Then you might want to testify to what God is doing in your life. Guess what? That is rebuilding.

Jesus was so adamant that the Sardians begin doing this that the word "strengthen" (*stērizo*), as it is used, focuses on the beginning of an action.[43] He wanted them to begin rebuilding their spiritual lives on the virtues that had survived. Right away. Like San Francisco, they didn't have time to waste. They had the material they needed and they could start construction right where they were, in the middle of their rubble.

Has your spiritual life been in shambles, even just a little? What things do you still have a conviction toward? What do you still believe in? *Those* are the things God wants you to practice this week. Don't focus on all the things that have been destroyed. Focus on what good you still have. Begin to give attention and care to those things, right away. When you do, you'll see the beginning of a spiritual renaissance taking place in your life.

PRAYER FOR THE WEEK

Dear Heavenly Father—
I thank You that You have given me a plan to help me rebuild. I ask
You for the power of Your Holy Spirit to give constant attention and
support to the things in my life that I still have a conviction toward.
May this revive my walk with You. I declare that You are rebuilding
me and that my relationship with You will be better than it ever has
been. In Jesus's name, amen!

ACTIVITY FOR THE WEEK

Strengthen your favorite spiritual discipline. Pick your favorite one—
reading God's Word, going to church, praying, singing, etc.— and put an
extra 30 minutes a day toward it.

SCRIPTURES FOR THE WEEK

Psalm 37:23–24

Proverbs 24:16

Matthew 7:24–27

Matthew 16:17–19

1 Corinthians 3:12–15

Ephesians 2:19–22

36

STAY CONNECTED TO
THE POWER

Wake up, and strengthen what remains and is about to die, for I have not found your works complete in the sight of my God.

(Revelation 3:2)

γίνου γρηγορῶν καὶ στήρισον τὰ λοιπὰ ἃ ἔμελλον ἀποθα-
νεῖν, οὐ γὰρ εὕρηκά σου τὰ ἔργα πεπληρωμένα ἐνώπιον
τοῦ θεοῦ μου.   (ΑΠΟΚΑΛΥΨΙΣ ΙΩΑΝΝΟΥ 3:2)

My clock died on August 14, 2003, around 4:15 p.m. I glanced at it while I was getting ready for work and the light suddenly vanished. *Great, just what I need,* I thought. *Eighty-seven degrees outside and now we don't have power.* Losing power in Michigan during the summer is a sticky situation—literally. The humidity soaks your clothes and they stick to your skin like old gum on blacktop. Little did I know, I wasn't the only one tugging on a dank, sweaty T-shirt—50 million other people were, too. It became known as the "Northeast Blackout of 2003." New York City, Detroit, Cleveland, and Newark, New Jersey, were among the cities affected, along with parts of Ontario, Canada.

It was a sheer mess that lasted, in some places, up to two days. One hundred related deaths were reported, due to fire, carbon monoxide poisoning, heart attack, and medical equipment failure. People were left stranded in subways, elevators, and even on roller coasters. Business owners suffered when their refrigerated stock spoiled. In New York City alone, the losses were estimated at $500 million. And, of course, people couldn't shower, charge their cellular phones, or go to the grocery store. It was a sobering time. It dawned on me how many things need power to operate and how dependent human life is on it. If the power grid goes down, the quality of life suffers in a devastating way.

> *Enōpion* ("in the sight of") is made up of two Greek words: *en* ("in") and *optánomai* ("to allow oneself to be seen"). It means to appear in the view of another.

In Revelation 3:2, Jesus tells the church in Sardis that the quality of their spiritual life was suffering. Things weren't the way they used to be and God had taken notice. Jesus says their works had not been found *"complete in the sight of my God."* The Greek word for "in the sight of" (*enōpion*) is a preposition that means "to be in front of something." It gives us the picture of the Sardian church standing in front of God while He observes them. As He does, He forms an opinion about what He sees them doing. Did you know God has an opinion of how you live your life? In the Sardians' case, it wasn't good. He didn't think their works cut it—they weren't up to His standards. And God had detected why: their power grid had gone down.

The power grid in the life of every believer is the Holy Spirit. He is the one who transmits and delivers the power of God into our everyday lives so we are able to produce godly works and live a life that meets God's standards. Jesus clearly taught that we couldn't live our Christian lives without the Holy Spirit (see Luke 24:49; Acts 1:8) and trying to do so saddens

God. (See Ephesians 4:30.) This is because the Holy Spirit is the only source of healings, miracles, deliverance, and salvation. (See 1 Corinthians 12:8–10.) When we consider the different revivals of the past and present that have led to the salvation and spiritual transformations of billions of people, it's always because of the work of the Holy Spirit. The Spirit led to the birth of the church and 3,000 salvations on the day of Pentecost. (See Acts 2:41.) He was the spark behind the Reformation of sixteenth century Europe. He was the engine that drove the First and Second Great Awakenings in 1727 and 1810. He was the wind in the sails of the Azusa Street Revival starting in 1906 and He continues to ignite hearts in all hemispheres today. We *must* have His power.

WE NEED HOLY SPIRIT POWER

Unfortunately, the Sardians didn't have it. Jesus told them their works were not "complete" (*poplērōmena*). In the Greek, this word means "to fill something up." It was used to describe filling a bottle to the top with water or filling an ewer completely full of wine. Having our works "complete" means they are totally filled with the presence and the power of the Spirit. When our works are saturated by the Spirit, they maintain the quality that God expects. That means our preaching and teaching are anointed, our evangelizing is backed by the supernatural gifts of the Spirit, our church services are lively and vibrant, and our lifestyle is full of the fruits of the Spirit. You wouldn't find this in Sardis. You'd find the majority of the church just *playing church*: saying the things they were supposed to say and acting rote without any fire for more of God. They were the product of human ability and not the Spirit's ability. The power grid had blown and they were without the Spirit. Therefore, the quality of their spirituality and their relationship with God had suffered.

Are you connected to the power grid? Does the Holy Spirit charge your life with His supply every day? The Spirit wants to send currents of His activity into everything you do. He wants you to go throughout your day beaming with His might and He wants you to radiate His energy when you pray for others and do the work of His kingdom. Take a lesson from the Sardians: God doesn't like works that are done without the power of His Spirit. This week, don't attempt to get by doing things from your own ability and cognition. Keep the power flowing and the quality of your works will please God.

PRAYER FOR THE WEEK

Dear Heavenly Father—
I need the power of the Holy Spirit in my life. I want Him to charge everything I do for Your kingdom. I cannot get by on my own abilities, and I cannot continue in my own strength. I don't want to play church nor do I want to be satisfied with where I am with You. I want more of You and I want more of Your Spirit. So, I surrender more of me. May your supernatural gifts flow into my life and may my service for the kingdom be saturated in Your power. In Jesus's name, amen!

ACTIVITY FOR THE WEEK

Read through the book of Acts. There are 28 chapters, so try to read four chapters a day and highlight or make note of every instance and demonstration of the Spirit's work. As you do, ask Him for His power and demonstration in your life and ministry.

SCRIPTURES FOR THE WEEK

Zechariah 4:6

Luke 14:18–19

Luke 24:49

Acts 1:8

Acts 4:33

Romans 15:19

37

A PAPER TIGER, DON'T BE

Remember, then, what you received and heard. Keep it, and repent. If you will not wake up, I will come like a thief, and you will not know at what hour I will come against you.

(Revelation 3:3)

μνημόνευε οὖν πῶς εἴληφας καὶ ἤκουσας καὶ τήρει καὶ μετανόησον. ἐὰν οὖν μὴ γρηγορήσῃς, ἥξω ὡς κλέπτης, καὶ οὐ μὴ γνῷς ποίαν ὥραν ἥξω ἐπὶ σέ.

(ΑΠΟΚΑΛΥΨΙΣ ΙΩΑΝΝΟΥ 3:3)

I was a paper tiger during my junior year of high school—someone who acts or talks fierce but can't land a claw. Know-it-alls often get this reputation. They are usually full of elaborate theories, statistics, and analyses, but they have nothing substantial—no impact—to back it up. This describes the extent of my fishing expertise when I was sixteen.

I had just caught my first pike right before fall turned into winter. Winters are cold in Michigan, which means no fishing. To feed my new addiction for the next five months, I subscribed to three angler magazines and stocked up on all of the fresh water fishing literature I could find. I was "hooked." I wasn't just studying the basics, like lure colors and tackle options. I was learning how barometric pressure influenced fish behavior; I was examining how to "structure fish." I was even figuring out how to use the phases of the moon to give my angling an advantage.

When the winter season was nearly over, you should have heard me talking to my older friends who had been fishing for years. I was chatting like the teacher, saying things like, "When there is surface structure, that's the perfect time to pull out the Zara spook and walk the dog" and "We should go out when a low-pressure system moves through. The fish will go on a feeding frenzy and that will really cause our rod tips to bend." They were amused. Everything I was saying was true. I just had no experience behind it.

Finally, the day came to get the lines wet. "Alright, Chris," Adam said. "Let's see you walk the dog with that spook." I pulled out my brand-new, shiny, nine-dollar lure, wound it back, and heard it snap off my line as it soared into the lake. I had tied it on wrong. I was now the joke of the evening. In fact, I even got shut out. My friends left up several fish and I left down a spook…all because I was the paper tiger with no experience.

In Revelation 3:3, Jesus reminds the dying Sardian church about the important role that experience plays in our spiritual lives. We can't thrive only on what we know; we have to *experience* what we know. God's Word calls this being a doer of the Word. (See James 1:22.) If we fail to experience the things we have learned, our spiritual lives will wither, no matter how much knowledge we've acquired.

To communicate this, Jesus says, *"Remember, then, what you received and heard"* (*mnēmoneue oun pōs eilēphas kai ēkousaskai*). "Received" (*eilēphas*) refers to "seizing and bringing into possession." Here, it is talking about the wonderful experiences that the believers in Sardis possessed from being connected to the ongoing work of the Holy Spirit. This would include the miracles they had been part of, the deliverances they had seen, the healings that God used them to minister—everything that had to do with kingdom work. What's interesting is that the things they received and experienced are mentioned *before* the things they heard ("received and heard"). It seems a little out of order because first we *hear* about the gospel *then* we *receive and experience* it, right?

> "Hysteron proteron" comes from the Greek words *husteron* ("arriving later") and *proteron* ("before").

STRESSED IMPORTANT IDEAS, YODA DID

It is actually out of order on purpose. This is a writing device called "hysteron proteron." It is a Greek expression that means "later earlier." Basically, the writer takes the word that should be last in order and puts it first to emphasize it. You employ this when you say, "I'm putting on my shoes and socks." You don't put your shoes on before your socks, do you? You likely just think your shoes are more important than your socks. Master Yoda from *Star Wars* always talked like this: "Mourn them, do not. Miss them, do not."[44] Grammatically, he should say, "Do not mourn them. Do not miss them." But he wanted to stress how important it was for Anakin not to mourn those who die and become part of the Force.

Power with the Holy Spirit, the Sardians had lost. Mighty demonstrations, they saw no longer. The move of God, a thing of the past. Knowledge, they took pride in. Grieved, was Jesus.

Jesus told them they needed to start remembering the things they had once received and experienced. Their community was to begin talking about the days of old when God moved with power in their church. A constant recollection of their experience would stir up the embers and produce the fire of the Spirit in their community once again. No longer were they just to take pride in what they *knew*. God wanted them to do some damage; He wanted them to be more than a paper tiger.

Are you demonstrating the things you have heard, or do those things merely stay in your memory? God wants you to move beyond what you know and into the realm of experience. This week, step out when the Holy Spirit gives you a leading. Pray for the sick. Minister salvation to the lost.

Take up an opportunity to defend your faith with someone who puts it down. You'll find that experiencing your faith is a notch above just knowing about it.

PRAYER FOR THE WEEK

Dear Heavenly Father—
I don't just want to be someone who knows about what I believe; I want
to be someone who lives it. I want to see, experience, and demonstrate
in my life. Holy Spirit, every day this week, use me in the power of God.
At the end of the week, I want a brand-new testimony from each day. I
declare my faith is dangerous, and it will do damage to the kingdom of
hell. In Jesus's name, amen!

ACTIVITY FOR THE WEEK

Record every instance where you experience the power of the Holy Spirit in your life this week. Keep a log for each day. At the end of the week, reflect. How alive is your faith? Is it more of what you know intellectually, or is the Spirit of God using you to demonstrate His kingdom in the earth?

SCRIPTURES FOR THE WEEK

Psalm 77:11	1 Timothy 4:14–16
Isaiah 46:9	2 Timothy 4:5
Jonah 2:7	Hebrews 10:32–36

38

GOD WANTS YOUR CLOTHES TO BE CLEAN

Yet you have still a few names in Sardis, people who have not soiled their garments, and they will walk with me in white, for they are worthy. The one who conquers will be clothed thus in white garments, and I will never blot his name out of the book of life. I will confess his name before my Father and before his angels. (Revelation 3:4–5)

ἀλλ᾽ ἔχεις ὀλίγα ὀνόματα ἐν Σάρδεσιν ἃ οὐκ ἐμόλυναν τὰ ἱμάτια αὐτῶν, καὶ περιπατήσουσιν μετ᾽ ἐμοῦ ἐν λευκοῖς, ὅτι ἄξιοί εἰσιν. ὁ νικῶν οὕτως περιβαλεῖται ἐν ἱματίοις λευκοῖς καὶ οὐ μὴ ἐξαλείψω τὸ ὄνομα αὐτοῦ ἐκ τῆς βίβλου τῆς ζωῆς καὶ ὁμολογήσω τὸ ὄνομα αὐτοῦ ἐνώπιον τοῦ πατρός μου καὶ ἐνώπιον τῶν ἀγγέλων αὐτοῦ.
(ΑΠΟΚΑΛΥΨΙΣ ΙΩΑΝΝΟΥ 3:4–5)

Illiam Nowell may have been the worst-smelling man in Los Angeles. His odor offended people, especially his neighbors. It was stale and stagnant, perhaps somewhat reminiscent of sour milk and mold. Whatever it was, they said it oozed through his apartment walls, gagged them, and saturated their possessions. More than once, cops showed up at Nowell's apartment to investigate complaints of a dead body stink wafting around. But there was no dead body. Nowell just refused to bathe, groom, or change clothes.

Before Nowell moved into his apartment, he had spent over twenty years living on the streets. He came into a $200,000 lawsuit settlement and had gotten the apartment of his dreams. But the ex-drifter didn't want to change his ways. He didn't wear shoes and his feet were said to look like "black claws." He never changed his pants. Norwell even rejected toiletries that his leasing agent purchased for him to use. After months of complaints, the apartment complex took him to court to have him evicted. He didn't stand a chance. Instead of grooming himself to look presentable, he showed up in his putrid clothes.

William Nowell was evicted. However, jury foreman Eric Andrist sympathized with him and tried to help him get an appeal. Andrist found a lawyer who would work with Nowell so long as he groomed and got new clothes. Nowell refused. When he tried to rent an apartment in another building, the owner told him no.

Dirty clothes are certain to cause rejection.

The concept of citizenship goes back to the city-states of ancient Greece. The city in which a person belonged was the foundation of their identity. Citizens pledged allegiance to their city, paid taxes, and were liable for military service. In return, they received protection and the right to vote.

In Revelation 3:4–5, Jesus tells the church at Sardis that many of them had soiled garments that were keeping them out of the presence of God. The Greek word for "soiled" (*molynō*) means "to smear with dirt; to spoil;

to defile." It was a word used to describe pigs that rolled around in the mud. It could accurately describe Nowell's clothes and it depicts attire you wouldn't want to wear if you had any respect for yourself. Imagine going to the gym for an intense workout and leaving your clothes in your gym bag overnight. Would you wear them to a meeting the next day? Of course not.

God's Word is telling us that if we want to live near the presence of God, we must keep our *garments holy and pure*. This refers to living a holy lifestyle that is governed by the power of the Holy Spirit and the Word of God. The Spirit and the Word work hand in hand to keep our lives washed and pure. (See Romans 12:1–2; Ephesians 5:26.) *Every time we go to God's Word and read it with the help and sensitivity of the Holy Spirit, it's like putting our mind and emotions in the washing machine. It churns, bubbles, and spins, so we come out smelling fresh and clean.*

HOW TO WALK WITH JESUS

Jesus says those who have clean garments will *"walk with me in white."* The Greek word "walk" (*peripateō*) often meant to have an immediate relationship with someone. To walk with someone often expressed close attachment, like the way in which Enoch walked with God. (See Genesis 5:24.) This tells us that the secret to being in the presence of God and living with Him is purity. It means not following Instagram pages that are full of sex, violence, and lewd humor. It means being honest on your taxes. It means not showing off your curves just to get a few likes.

For the people who do this, Jesus says, *"I will never blot his name out of the book of life"* (*ou mē exaleipsō autou to onoma ek tēs biblou tēs zōēs*). The idea of a book of life comes from a registry of citizens, like the one in ancient Athens. When a criminal was executed for a crime, their name was expunged from the book. Jesus was telling his holy saints that they never had to worry about this happening. They can look forward to living in the presence of God forever. In fact, everything about this statement is emphatic. First, Jesus uses the emphatic words for "never" (*ou mē*). This is like saying, "Never, never!"

Second, this statement is what is known as a *litotes*, when an affirmative is expressed by a negative for emphasis. Jesus could have said, "I'll keep his name in the book of life." But instead He said, "I will never blot out his name out of the book of life." It's an ironic understatement. Like when someone asks how your day is and instead of saying "good" you say, "Not bad!" Usually, "not bad" means "more than good." All this goes to show that Jesus was being very reassuring to His holy saints that they never had to worry about being evicted from the presence of God. God welcomes those who live lives of purity in His midst. But those who refuse to adjust their lifestyle, like William Nowell, are headed for rejection.

While we all have made mistakes and have come short of God's glory (see Romans 3:23), the Holy Spirit gives us the power we need to clean up our act so we can live our lives in the presence of God. While God's grace cleans us up, we have to be *willing* to let Him help us. We can't refuse grooming. Today, no matter what you've done, let the Spirit of God make you clean. Let Him prepare you to live in the presence of God forever.

PRAYER FOR THE WEEK

Dear Heavenly Father—
I want to be clean and pure. I want to live in Your presence forever. I thank You that Your precious Holy Spirit can wash the stink right off of me. I pray that Your Word will fill my heart and life and continually cleanse me, enabling me to walk closer and closer to You. Thank You that the Holy Spirit is at work in my life and that You will never evict me from Your presence. In Jesus's name, amen!

ACTIVITY FOR THE WEEK

Do some cleaning. Wash your car, scrub your bathroom, fold some laundry, or take a brisk shower. As you do, worship God for making you clean. Ask Him to purify every area of your life. What are some areas of your life that you want Him to scrub? Are there any patterns of thinking you want Him to bleach?

SCRIPTURES FOR THE WEEK

Psalm 51:7   John 15:3

Ezekiel 36:25   1 Corinthians 6:11

Ephesians 5:26   Hebrews 10:22

PART VII

THE CHURCH AT PHILADELPHIA—STUDIES ON CHRISTIAN LIVING

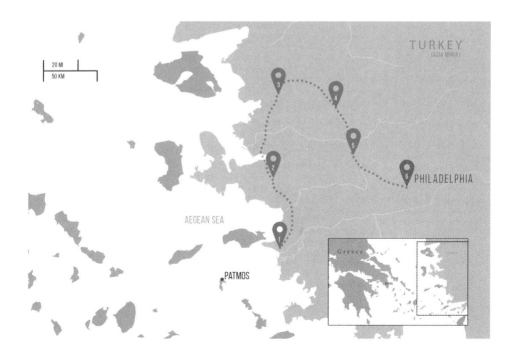

39

GOD'S ENDORSEMENT IS ALL YOU NEED

And to the angel of the church in Philadelphia write: The words of the holy one, the true one, who has the key of David, who opens and no one will shut, who shuts and no one opens.

(Revelation 3:7)

Καὶ τῷ ἀγγέλῳ τῆς ἐν Φιλαδελφείᾳ ἐκκλησίας γράψον Τάδε λέγει ὁ ἅγιος, ὁ ἀληθινός, ὁ ἔχων τὴν κλεῖν Δαυίδ, ὁ ἀνοίγων καὶ οὐδεὶς κλείσει καὶ κλείων καὶ οὐδεὶς ἀνοί-γει. (ΑΠΟΚΑΛΥΨΙΣ ΙΩΑΝΝΟΥ 3:7)

Airbnb has become quite a threat to the hotel industry. Founded in 2008, it is an option for lodgers in 191 countries and currently has over four million listings. If you aren't familiar with Airbnb, it is an industry-disrupting online platform that enables its users to book lodging in ordinary residences of other people. Researchers studied prices and occupancy rates in fifty major U.S. cities between 2011 and 2014 to compare how Airbnb was affecting hotels. The research showed that Airbnb had reduced hotel profits by 3.7 percent in the ten largest cities where it had a presence. Airbnb continues to succeed today, despite the hotel industry's efforts to fight back and lobby for more government regulation of the home-sharing site.

Billionaire hedge-fund owner, Warren Buffet, plays a small but interesting role in Airbnb's success. Every year, Buffet's hedge fund, *Berkshire Hathaway*, has its annual conference in Buffet's hometown, Omaha, Nebraska. Over 30,000 shareholders travel to Omaha for the event. The hotel industry was taking advantage of the situation by price gouging, with some hotels doubling and even tripling their prices. Buffet felt responsible and wanted to protect his shareholders, so he endorsed Airbnb. He suggested that his shareholders consider using it for lodging and he suggested to Airbnb that they look into expanding their number of hosts to accommodate the incoming shareholders. As a result, Airbnb more than doubled its listings in Omaha and gained more stature because of Buffet's endorsement.

Nobody can stop your success if you are backed by the right person. In Revelation 3:7, the church at Philadelphia learned they had the right person backing them. In spite of their persecutors, they were certain to fulfill God's plan for their lives because Jesus was more powerful than their haters.

Hating on the Philadelphian church were the Jewish zealots similar to the ones in Smyrna. (See Revelation 2:9.) Among their sharp assaults, these Jews had been telling the Philadelphia believers that Jesus was not the Messiah and they were not going to enter the messianic kingdom. Only *they*, and *not* the Jesus followers, were going to access the kingdom.

JESUS OFFERS US THE REAL DEAL

Hearing this over and over again would have been disheartening. But Jesus came to encourage His followers. He wanted them to be certain that their destiny didn't hang on what the Jews said or did. His support was all they needed. So, He first announces to them who He is: *"the holy one, the true one, who has the key of David, who opens and no one will shut…"* (*ho hagios ho alēthinos ho echōn tēn klein Dauid ho anoigōn kai oudeis kleisei*).

The structure of this sentence is very interesting. It is called an asyndeton, a literary device that eliminates conjunctions, such as "and," "but," and "or," to speed up the rhythm of words and create a powerful impact. This is one way that ancient authors underlined and bolded words. It underscored the immensity of the one backing the Philadelphian church.

> "Alethiology" (*alētheia* meaning "truth" and *logía* meaning "study") is the "study of truth." It is similar to *epistemology* (*epistēmē* meaning "knowledge"), the "study of knowledge."

Within the powerful description of Himself, Jesus says He is the one who is "true" (*alēthinos*). This means "genuine." The Philadelphians had the real deal backing them. To prove this, Jesus says He has the key of David. This is a reference to Eliakim's authority in Isaiah 22:15–25. Isaiah heard God say that Eliakim would have "the key of the house David." This meant Eliakim would become King Hezekiah's new chief steward over the royal treasure and access to the treasure would come through him. (See Isaiah 22:20–25.) Jesus used this term because *He* is the authority over the riches of the kingdom and access to them comes only through Him. This meant the Philadelphian believers had the right person on their side. Their persecutors could not stop their entrance into the kingdom because they served the one with all power and authority…and He had their backs.

It's important for you to understand you will never have *everyone* on your side when you are working to accomplish the will of God. You'll always have enemies and naysayers who will seek your demise. Their criticisms are usually harsh and belittling; they will often tell you how far from the will of God you are. You may take a new job and they tell you the job isn't good for you. You might become engaged to a wonderful and godly mate, but they'll tell you everything that is wrong with that person. Don't listen if they are only out to spite God's purpose. You don't need them. On your side, you have the genuine, the true, the one who backs you—the God who gives you access to His riches when everyone else tries to deny your path. Mourn not those against you. Rejoice in the one whose endorsement you have.

PRAYER FOR THE WEEK

Dear Heavenly Father—
I thank You and praise You that my opponents cannot block Your will for my life. So long as I have Your endorsement, I will succeed in the things You have called me to do. Holy Spirit, I pray You continue to give me access into the glorious riches that have been laid aside for me in Christ. May every grace abound in my life so I can finish the course You have set before me in spite of every obstacle. In Jesus's name, amen!

ACTIVITY FOR THE WEEK

Get God's endorsement. Make a list of everything in your life that you are working to accomplish. Did God tell you to do these things? Do you have His endorsement on them? Pray about it. If God tells you that you have His backing, sign *God* next to these things. When times get difficult, pull out the list and remind yourself who is behind you.

SCRIPTURES FOR THE WEEK

Proverbs 16:7	2 Corinthians 5:9
Mark 3:33–35	Galatians 1:10
Acts 5:29	Ephesians 6:6–7

40

WAIT FOR GOD'S OPPORTUNITIES TO CHANGE YOUR LIFE

...who opens and no one will shut, who shuts and no one opens. I know your works. Behold, I have set before you an open door, which no one is able to shut. (Revelation 3:7b–8a)

...ὁ ἀνοίγων καὶ οὐδεὶς κλείσει καὶ κλείων καὶ οὐδεὶς ἀνοί-γει Οἶδά σου τὰ ἔργα, ἰδοὺ δέδωκα ἐνώπιόν σου θύραν ἠνεῳγμένην, ἣν οὐδεὶς δύναται κλεῖσαι αὐτην.
(ΑΠΟΚΑΛΥΨΙΣ ΙΩΑΝΝΟΥ 3:7b–8a)

On January 25, 2004, NASA's *Opportunity* rover touched down onto the dusty surface of Mars and began its highly anticipated mission. It was supposed to last only 92 earth days, but *Opportunity* more than lived up to its name. It was still going strong until June 2018, when a severe Martian dust storm caused it to stop communicating with Earth. *Opportunity* had tracked over 28 miles on Mars and accomplished some pretty amazing things. It spent two years studying the Victoria crater, detected argon, gave plausible evidence that water was once indigenous to Mars, and sent back plenty of atmospheric data.

One fascinating fact about *Opportunity* is how it got its name. NASA held a nationwide essay contest to name the rover and over 10,000 people submitted entries. Nine-year-old Sofi Collis from Arizona won. Before she came to America, Sofi grew up in a Siberian orphanage and used to dream of living in the U.S. Her essay was only fifty words long but she was still able to capture what America had done for her: "I used to live in an orphanage. It was dark and cold and lonely. At night I would look up and see the sky and I felt better. Thank you for the *spirit* and the *opportunity*." Asked about her essay, she said, "Well, you couldn't really do anything at the orphanage. But when you come to America, you can do whatever you want to do and be whatever you want to be and that was spirit and opportunity." Sofi had learned the power of opportunity at a younger age than most. An opportunity can change everything when it comes along—including space exploration and an orphan's life.

"Philadelphia" (*philos* meaning "love" and *adelphos* meaning "brother") means "brotherly love." This biblical city is said to have been founded in the second century B.C. by the Pergamum King Eumenes II and named after the love he had for his brother, Attalus II.

JESUS CONTROLS OUR OPPORTUNITIES

In Revelation 3:7–8, Jesus brings an opportunity for the church in Philadelphia that would eventually change everything: deliverance from those who had been persecuting them and access into His kingdom. Hearing this would have invigorated the small church of faithful believers who had been patiently waiting for God to intervene. When presenting the opportunity, Jesus alludes to a door, saying He is the one *"who opens and no one will shut, who shuts and no one opens"* (*ho anoigōn kai oudeis kleisei kai kleiōn kai oudeis anoigei*). This statement packs a punch because it is a *chiasmus*, a repetition of an idea in reverse sequence. We use this in English all of the time when we want to forcefully drive home a point. We say, "We work to live, not live to work." Or, think of President John F. Kennedy's famous line, "Ask not what your country can do for you, ask what you can do for your country." The play on the words adds emphasis and creates even bigger ideas beyond the words stated.

"We work to live, not live to work" means work is not the point of life. Jesus's statement has its own theme: ultimately, *the Lord* is in control of our opportunities. In His timing, He creates them for us. Toiling and trying in our own strength will only tire us out and leave us frustrated and confused. Victorious Christian living means trusting God to create the right opportunities for us and having patience until those opportunities come along. It also means not trying to create change by yourself.

Have you tried to change your life in your own strength by creating your own opportunities that God had nothing to do with? Maybe you jumped the gun on dating by going out with a total jerk that God didn't send your way. Perhaps you got into ministry before the Lord said, "Go," and ended up embarrassed and disappointed. As an international teacher, I was disappointed that I never had the opportunity to go anywhere in Asia. I had a tremendous desire to go. I had tried setting up opportunities on my own for years, but they always fell apart. One Sunday morning, as I was preparing to preach, I had a sudden, expected vision from the Lord: I was in Asia helping the underground church. I sensed the Lord was saying it was time to go. Two weeks later, the Lord connected me to an individual who opened up the entire continent to me. In just one year, I visited seven Asian countries and I didn't even have to try. The Opportunity Maker said it was time. That's all it took.

This week, trust that your life will be filled with opportunities from the Lord. Instead of losing your focus trying to drum them up yourself, stay sensitive to the Holy Spirit so you can recognize when something from Him *actually* comes along. *These* are the opportunities you want to jump on because one opportunity from *God* can change *everything*.

PRAYER FOR THE WEEK

Dear Heavenly Father—
I thank You that opportunities come from You. I don't want to try to
make things happen on my own. I've tried that already, Lord, and it
is frustrating and tiresome. Holy Spirit, give me the patience I need to
wait for God's doors to open before me, give me the discernment I need
to recognize them, and give me the boldness I need to go through them.
In Jesus's name, amen!

ACTIVITY FOR THE WEEK

Think about different opportunities that have come along in your life.
Which ones were from God and which ones weren't? Pick one that God
created and one that you created. Compare them. Did they feel different?
Did you sense grace or a lack thereof? Jot down some key things that distinguish divine opportunities from opportunities we create ourselves.

SCRIPTURES FOR THE WEEK

1 Samuel 2:9	Psalm 37:4–5, 23
Psalm 20:4	Psalm 145:19
Psalm 25:12	1 Corinthians 16:8–9

41

GOD IS HOLDING THE DOOR FOR YOU

I know your works. Behold, I have set before you an open door, which no one is able to shut. (Revelation 3:8a)

Οἶδά σου τὰ ἔργα, ἰδοὺ δέδωκα ἐνώπιόν σου θύραν ἠνεῳγμένην, ἣν οὐδεὶς δύναται κλεῖσαι αὐτήν.
(ΑΠΟΚΑΛΥΨΙΣ ΙΩΑΝΝΟΥ 3:8a)

If you know who Wayne Williams is, you don't have to be a baseball fan to appreciate the 2016 World Series. Wayne, who was sixty-eight at the time, lived in North Carolina and was a die-hard Chicago Cubs fan. When he was just a young boy, he and his father promised each other that when the Cubs reached the World Series, they would listen to the games together.

A simple enough promise. But the Cubs didn't make it to the World Series in his father's lifetime. His dad passed away in 1980.

Yet, in 2016—thirty-six years after Wayne's father died—the Cubs got in. The best of seven series stretched as far as it could and was about to go into a seventh and decisive game. That's when Wayne packed up his car and drove from North Carolina to Indianapolis to keep his end of the long-time promise: he was going to listen to the ball game next to his father's grave.

Reporters showed up to cover the story. The picture they took will yank the tears right from your eyes: quad chair set up, Cubs attire on, alone in the dark cemetery with just a small flashlight to illuminate the headstone of the grave, Wayne Williams sat there keeping his promise to his beloved father—a promise that was made over four decades earlier.

Promises are as good as those who make them. And when faithful people make them, time and circumstances have no bearing upon their coming to pass. A promise is a promise.

NO ONE CAN SHUT JESUS'S DOOR

In Revelation 3:8, the church in Philadelphia learned that Jesus is a faithful promise-keeper. In fact, He's so faithful that the persecution and acute difficulty they faced could not prevent His promises from coming to fruition. This is what He is telling the Philadelphian church when He says, *"Behold, I have set before you an open door, which no one is able to shut."*

> *Thyra* is the Greek word for "door." In Greco-Roman days, some shields were shaped like doors and, therefore, called *thyreos*. "Thyroid," a derivative of *thyra*, is a shield-shaped gland.

The Greek word "set" (*dedōka*) means "to give a promised gift." The door of opportunity that Jesus placed before the Philadelphian church was a promise that they would rule and reign with Him when He returned. This would include total deliverance from their persecutors. Set (*dedōka*) is also found in a tense that takes place in the past, with its results continuing on into the future.[45] This means that once Jesus had set this promised door before them, it stayed open. Actually, Jesus is the one holding the door open. He was assuring the church that no matter what transpired until that time, the door would stay open and His promise to them would be good. Just like a gentleman, God holds the doors of His promises open to us. If you desire to get through, He will make sure the circumstances of life don't cause the door to slam in your face.

All of us are carrying a promise from God that has afforded us an opportunity to be part of His kingdom. We must remember that ultimately, Jesus is the one who is going to make sure that these promises come to pass. Even if we get off track and waste time, we have a faithful God. Just as Wayne Williams didn't let death end the vow he had made to his father, Jesus won't let the circumstances of life shut the promises He has made to you.

I remember when God told me I'd teach His Word from the Greek. I immediately became discouraged and sulked because I'd hardly paid any attention to Greek in my undergraduate studies. I blew off the classes I was required to take and didn't take advantage of the advanced classes the university was offering. I figured I was ruined and had missed my chance before I even got started. I thought, *Teach from the Greek? Lord, didn't you see me skipping undergrad classes?*

But lo and behold, God led me to a seminary to begin my graduate studies and placed two wonderful professors into my life. They not only taught me advanced Greek, but drove an even deeper love for God's Word in me that I hadn't had earlier! I don't think I would have appreciated these professors as much in my undergrad years; I was too immature. The point is that God promised me I would teach from the Greek and, despite my immaturity, He held the door open and made sure I got through.

What door of opportunity has God promised to you? Have you wasted time instead of entering? Are the circumstances of life blocking you from going through? If so, this week, it's important to remember that Jesus is going to hold that door for you as long as you are serious about going through. He is the one who made the promise and He remains faithful when we aren't. (See 2 Timothy 2:13.) Keep going and ask Him to help push you through. After all, it's His promise…and a promise is a promise.

PRAYER FOR THE WEEK

Dear Heavenly Father—
I thank You for every opportunity that You have planned for my good
and have called me to enter. I realize that at times I can become weak,
distracted, and end up wasting time. But I ask You now to strengthen
me with Your Holy Spirit. Give me the power and grace to fight every
hindrance and enter the promise You have made for my life. In Jesus's
name, amen!

ACTIVITY FOR THE WEEK

Go through some doors. Every time you enter through a doorway, as
often as you can, say, "I declare I enter every promise God has made to me!"
Watch how it builds your faith.

SCRIPTURES FOR THE WEEK

Genesis 28:15	Romans 3:3–4
Numbers 23:19	2 Timothy 2:13
Deuteronomy 7:9	Hebrews 6:18

42

JUMP ONTO THE SHOULDERS OF ADVERSITY

I know that you have but little power, and yet you have kept my word and have not denied my name. (Revelation 3:8b)

ὅτι μικρὰν ἔχεις δύναμιν καὶ ἐτήρησάς μου τὸν λόγον καὶ οὐκ ἠρνήσω τὸ ὄνομά μου.
(ΑΠΟΚΑΛΥΨΙΣ ΙΩΑΝΝΟΥ 3:8b)

A**ll my life, I've grown up identifying as a Michigan Wolverine. It's a special feeling to put on the maize and blue, travel to Ann Arbor, and enter the Big House—the largest stadium in North America—to hail the victors with all of the other Wolverine fans. Yet, in all my years of being a devotee, I never realized until recently just how vicious an actual wolverine is.

A wolverine's Latin, scientific name is *gulo* which means "glutton." This comes from its reputation of being a ravenous eater. It will basically prey on

213

anything—deer, caribou, mountain goats, moose, you name it. In fact, you can watch YouTube videos of wolverines jumping onto the backs of much larger prey and shredding their shoulders until they dropped dead. Not bad for an animal that weighs an average of forty pounds. It may be small, but it has razor-sharp claws and powerful jaws that can hack through bone and tear frozen flesh.

Perhaps what makes a wolverine so dreaded is its attitude: it doesn't seem to fear much. If it wants something, it takes it. It's even been reported that a thirty-pound wolverine had the guts to try steal a kill from a 400 to 500-pound black bear! It didn't care that the bear was over ten times its size. Wolverines serve as nature's proof that size is apparently a state of mind. You can stand up to something much larger if it gets in the way of what you're after—*just as long as you have the right spirit in you.*

In Revelation 3:8, Jesus commends the spirit that the Philadelphian church had in them. Like a wolverine after its prey, they were in intense pursuit of the will of God for their lives. They desired to follow Christ and be part of His kingdom and none of their challenges or opponents were going to stop them.

> "Micro" comes from the Greek word *mikros*. Today, micro means "extremely small." Think of "microchip," "microscopic," and "microscope."

Yet, it's interesting that Jesus tells the Philadelphians they have "*little power*" (*mikran dynamin*). It seems insulting until we consider what it means. Here, "little" (*mikros*) means "insignificant" and "power" (*dynamis*) means "resources, supply." The church at Philadelphia was a small community and had few assets and resources; it's plausible they had no influential or rich individuals within their congregation. They were totally outnumbered by their opponents, which might have been a rational reason to be intimidated. Have you ever been around people who are in a higher financial and social league than you are? Imagine how it would feel if they *didn't* like you—and wanted to kill you.

CHURCH WAS SMALL BUT BOLD

Insignificant as the Philadelphian church might have been, the church didn't allow themselves to be intimidated; they didn't fear their opponents. They stood up to them. Jesus says, *"…and yet you have kept my word and have not denied my name."* This is telling how bold the Philadelphians were.

The verbs "kept" (*etērēsas*) and "denied" (*ērnēsō*) are both in a tense that denotes a specific occasion that took place in the past.[46] There had been very specific instances when the Philadelphian believers had been confronted and challenged by their much bigger opponents. Instead of backing down, the little group of believers in Philadelphia, like a wolverine, boldly met their match. They had their hearts and minds upon the kingdom of God. And they didn't care how small they were; they stood their ground and pushed back.

"[You] *have not denied my name"* is another litotes, an ironic understatement for emphasis and effect. (See chapter 38.) Jesus was emphatically saying, "You confessed My name!" He was overjoyed that the Philadelphians stood up to their opponents, even though they were outmatched in size. This demonstrated their faith in God and attested that they had God's mighty spirit in them.

God's Word tells us that He has not given us the spirit of fear but of power, love, and self-control. (See 2 Timothy 1:7.) If we are going to fulfill the purpose that God has for our lives, we can't back down when we seem outmatched or outnumbered. There will be moments in your life when you face adversity and the Holy Spirit inside of you will urge you to rise to the occasion. Will you cower in fear, measuring the outward appearances? Or will you jump onto the shoulders of the adversity, like the wolverine, and bring it down to the ground? God has placed His mighty Spirit in you— look forward to the outcome of your battles.

PRAYER FOR THE WEEK

Dear Heavenly Father—
You never promised that life would be easy. In fact, You tell us in John 16:33 that there will be many kinds of troubles. But many of Your greatest servants overcame the most overwhelming of odds. Holy Spirit,

it doesn't matter the size of the opponent—as long as You are in me,
I can overcome. Therefore, I will not be intimidated by my foes. I will
rise to every occasion and meet my challenges head-on because greater
is He that is in me than he that is in the world. In Jesus's name, amen!

ACTIVITY FOR THE WEEK

Meet your opponent head-on. What is the most intimidating thing in your life? Prepare to face it. Each day, pray over it until you sense the power of God taking hold of that thing in your life. As you pray, you will sense God putting His strength into you. Once you sense it's time to face it, don't hesitate—do what the Lord leads to do with boldness and confidence.

SCRIPTURES FOR THE WEEK

Exodus 23:22

Deuteronomy 31:6

Psalm 138:7

Philippians 1:28

2 Timothy 1:7

Hebrews 13:6

43

PEOPLE WILL HONOR YOU FOR FOLLOWING THE TRUTH

Behold, I will make those of the synagogue of Satan who say that they are Jews and are not, but lie—behold, I will make them come and bow down before your feet, and they will learn that I have loved you.   (Revelation 3:9)

ἰδοὺ διδῶ ἐκ τῆς συναγωγῆς τοῦ Σατανᾶ τῶν λεγόντων ἑαυτοὺς Ἰουδαίους εἶναι, καὶ οὐκ εἰσὶν ἀλλὰ ψεύδονται. ἰδοὺ ποιήσω αὐτοὺς ἵνα ἥξουσιν καὶ προσκυνήσουσιν ἐνώπιον τῶν ποδῶν σου καὶ γνῶσιν ὅτι ἐγὼ ἠγάπησά σε.
(ΑΠΟΚΑΛΥΨΙΣ ΙΩΑΝΝΟΥ 3:9)

Recognition doesn't come without a price. Unfortunately, everything that is good and true and right isn't immediately accepted with open arms and warm hugs. Quite the contrary. Following the truth wherever it leads has cost people a great deal of grief for long periods of time. Take Subrahmanyan Chandrasekhar, who won the Nobel Prize for Physics in 1983…long after he made his contribution to physics.

As a young man, Chandrasekhar had an intense interest in astrophysics. His brilliance led to a scholarship at Cambridge when he was twenty. In 1930, while on his way to Cambridge from his home in British India (Pakistan), he came up with what is known today as the Chandrasekhar limit: the maximum mass of a stable white dwarf star. If a star is above this mass, gravity will eventually collapse it into a black hole. (Don't feel bad if you don't understand this; I don't either.)

When Chandrasekhar presented his research at the Royal Astronomical Society in London in 1935, he was ridiculed and publicly embarrassed by his mentor, Sir Arthur Eddington, one of the great astrophysicists of the era. This wasn't good for Chandrasekhar's research or career. His idea became so unpopular that he eventually had to leave Cambridge. But in 1972, something phenomenal happened: the first black hole was discovered—and Chandrasekhar was vindicated. It took over thirty years for the world of science to see that Eddington was wrong and Chandrasekhar was correct, but the latter eventually earned a Nobel and astrophysicists have come to respect the Chandrasekhar limit.

In Revelation 2:9, Jesus tells the Philadelphian church that their Jewish persecutors were eventually going to honor them for following Him, the true Messiah. He cared about their well-being and was going to make sure the Philadelphians eventually got the respect they deserved for being faithful to His name.

JESUS PROMISES SPECIAL HONORS

Jesus says, *"I will make them come and bow down before your feet."* The Greek word for "bow down" (*proskyneō*) means "to show special honor; to welcome respectfully." Imagine how you are treated at your own birthday party or wedding. *You* are the honored guest: people bring gifts and cards, shower you with hugs and kisses, and toast to your name. God was assuring the Philadelphians that, sometime in the future, they would be celebrated by their persecutors.

The Jews were expecting the opposite, though. They thought the nations were going to come to *them* and bow down before *their* feet, based on prophecies. (See Isaiah 45:14; 49:23.) But Jesus was turning the tables. God makes sure that the ones who follow His truth end up with the honor. And Jesus tells the Philadelphian believers, *"They will learn that I have loved you."*

"Ego" is a person's sense of self-worth. It comes from the Greek word *egō*, meaning "I."

Here, the Greek word *ego* appears here for "I." *Egō* is an emphatic way of saying "I." It's like Jesus was saying, "When I turn the tables on them, they will see that I, *the true Messiah*, am on your side!" Believe it or not, God honors us for following Him. He values our commitment and loyalty to His name. At some point, He goes public with that honor and promotes us so those around us see that we've been living the truth. It delights God to vindicate His servants with open demonstrations of His love and grace.

Following God's truth may not be popular right now. Your beliefs and lifestyle may have caused some kinks at work, in your relationships, or at school. Maybe a boss has taken aim to interrupt your career. Perhaps your spouse has become furious at your continued commitment to serve the Lord. Whatever the case may be, remember, God is faithful to honor your faithfulness. That means you don't need to promote yourself. In His own timing, God will promote you. He will demonstrate to everyone that He loves you and that the truth you've been pursuing all this time has been right. Sooner or later, people will come to respect how you serve the Lord with your life.

PRAYER FOR THE WEEK

Dear Heavenly Father—
I thank You that You are the one who promotes me above my enemies and assures me that my walk with You gets the respect it deserves. I pray for my enemies: may they see that the truth I hold in You is real. Demonstrate Your love for me in front of them so they might know

Your truth as well. Thank You that my faithfulness to You doesn't go unrecognized by You. In Jesus's name, amen!

ACTIVITY FOR THE WEEK

Make a list for God to vindicate. What things are you saying or doing that your enemies tell you are wrong? List those things out and place the name of each respective person beside them. Begin praying for the Lord to reveal the truth about the matter to each person by placing special grace and favor upon your life for them to witness.

SCRIPTURES FOR THE WEEK

Deuteronomy 28:1

1 Samuel 2:30

Psalm 18:20

Psalm 91:5

Proverbs 4:7–8

John 12:26

44

PLAY BY GOD'S RULES

I am coming soon. Hold fast *what you have, so that no one may seize your crown.*   (Revelation 3:11)

ἔρχομαι ταχύ· κράτει ὃ ἔχεις, ἵνα μηδεὶς λάβῃ τὸν στέφα-νόν σου.   (ΑΠΟΚΑΛΥΨΙΣ ΙΩΑΝΝΟΥ 3:11)

The Olympics has had its fair share of cheaters since the Games began in 776 B.C. Fred Lorz, the marathon runner in the 1904 St. Louis games, may have been the most outlandish. That year, the race course was 24.85 miles. Runners not only had to overcome the distance, but 90-degree heat and perilous terrain. They were not expected to fare well, Lorz included.

After nine miles of running, Lorz began to suffer cramps. But he thought of an idea: *why not hitch a ride in an automobile.* For 11 miles, the marathon runner cruised past other runners and waved at them with a grin. When his cramps had subsided, Lorz got out of the car and completed the race. He reached the finish line in under three hours, ahead of everyone else. Unaware of his scheme, fans roared. President Theodore Roosevelt's twenty-year-old daughter placed a wreath on Lorz and was just about to lower the gold medal upon his neck when someone shouted that he was a cheater and exposed his rule-breaking. Boos ensued. Lorz insisted he had done it as a joke.

Cheating has always been looked upon with disgust. In the ancient Olympics, the penalties for cheating included flogging, seizing of property, and heavy fines. The money from these fines was often used to erect statues outside of the stadiums. In hopes of keeping the games honest, these figures warned contestants about the shame that comes from cheating. You can still see the remains of these statues today in Olympia, Greece. It doesn't matter which century or millennia you are from, cheating is never a good option. It is plumb ugly and it's certain to disqualify you.

> The "Zanes of Olympia" were bronze statues of Zeus that were paid for by Olympic athletes who were caught cheating. For further humiliation, the cheaters' names were inscribed on the bases of the statues.

Revelation 3:11 encourages the Philadelphian church to finish living their Christian lives with integrity and uprightness. They had gone a long distance holding onto their faith and testimony for Christ, and the Lord didn't want them to disqualify themselves before they reached the finish line. So, Jesus says, *"Hold fast what you have."*

PRESS PAST FUTURE DIFFICULTIES

The Greek word "hold fast" (*kratei*) is found in a manner that makes it come off as a strong insisting.[47] Jesus says it this way because there was more difficulty ahead for the Philadelphian church. He was acting as a coach or a trainer, urging them to press past the difficulty ahead and maintain their loving ways, spiritual growth, and the gifts and graces of the Spirit.

Jesus's strong encouragement was necessary because, despite their honorableness up to this point, it was still possible for them to break the rules and forfeit their reward. This is indicated by *"so that no one may seize your crown,"* a metaphorical statement alluding to the shameful penalty of cheating. Just as Fred Lorz's wreath and medal were revoked, so too could the Philadelphians' reward be revoked if they decided to cut corners and do things the wrong way when trials arose.

Life is full of temptations. Living in the will of God means doing things the *right way*, even when times are tough. Satan will always give you a corner to cut and will try to convince you why you should snip it off. He'll try to get you to feel sorry for yourself and make you feel like nobody is looking out for you except you. Then, you'll end up feeling "entitled" and thinking you have to do what you need to do to get by. What he doesn't say, though, is that this may disqualify you from experiencing some of the greatest blessings that God intends for you to have.

One afternoon, just recently, I was making a withdrawal from the bank. The teller handed me $20 extra. She probably had something else on her mind. I thought *today is your lucky day, Chris.* In just a second, I added up my difficulties, trying to figure out why I deserved this little extra cash. But I snapped out of it and handed it back to the teller. Of course, she was thankful because she could have gotten in trouble for her mistake. I had an opportunity to cut a corner…but is any amount of cash worth disobeying God's will for my life? God has a reward for me; I don't want anything to disqualify me from it. On the way out of the bank, I reminded the Lord that *He* is my provider and I don't have to cheat to accomplish His will for my life. God still takes care of me, every single day, with blessing upon blessing—many of them greater than I could ever imagine.

This week, don't cut any corners. If you have the opportunity to take advantage of someone's misfortune or if you can get away with something dishonest, refrain. Remind yourself that being in God's will means playing by God's rules. When you play by His rules, you'll always be able to look forward to honor, not shame.

PRAYER FOR THE WEEK

Dear Heavenly Father—
I never want to cut corners. I don't have to, because You are the one who makes Your will happen in my life. I declare that I am staying in the center of Your will, even when difficulties ensue. I will not allow

temptations to disqualify me from the reward You have set before me. Holy Spirit, give me the strength to continue living my life in a manner that brings honor to the Lord no matter the circumstances. I look forward to receiving the reward You have for me. That's far greater than anything I'd have to cheat to get. In Jesus's name, amen!

ACTIVITY FOR THE WEEK

Make things right. Have you gained anything the wrong way? Have you cut a corner somehow? If it's still possible, fix it. Be honest with those you've been dishonest with, return anything you've stolen, apologize to anyone you've besmirched. It will take boldness, but trust that after you do this, the Holy Spirit will bless your life in a way He never has before.

SCRIPTURES FOR THE WEEK

1 Kings 3:6   Proverbs 2:7

Psalm 15:1–2   Ephesians 5:15–16

Psalm 84:11   1 John 1:7

45

PEACE AND SECURITY COME FROM THE PRESENCE OF GOD

The one who conquers, I will make him a pillar *in the temple of my God. Never shall he go out of it, and I will write on him the* name *of my God, and the* name *of the city of my God, the new Jerusalem, which comes down from my God out of heaven, and my own new* name. (Revelation 3:12)

ὁ νικῶν ποιήσω αὐτὸν στῦλον ἐν τῷ ναῷ τοῦ θεοῦ μου καὶ ἔξω οὐ μὴ ἐξέλθη ἔτι καὶ γράψω ἐπ' αὐτὸν τὸ ὄνομα τοῦ θεοῦ μου καὶ τὸ ὄνομα τῆς πόλεως τοῦ θεοῦ μου, τῆς καινῆς Ἰερουσαλὴμ ἡ καταβαίνουσα ἐκ τοῦ οὐρανοῦ ἀπὸ τοῦ θεοῦ μου, καὶ τὸ ὄνομά μου τὸ καινόν.

(ΑΠΟΚΑΛΥΨΙΣ ΙΩΑΝΝΟΥ 3:12)

Selfitis is a behavior that psychologists have become serious about studying. Though not officially classified as a mental disorder (yet), selfitis has become known as "the obsessive-compulsive desire to take photos of one's self and post them on social media as a way to make up for a lack of self-esteem and fill a gap in intimacy." The research done thus far has indicated that those with selfitis were more likely to take selfies to feel good, show off, and compete with others to get more "likes." While posting a selfie or two certainly doesn't mean one has selfitis, there are studies that suggest some people do show signs of selfie addiction, more or less.

Danny Bowman is one of them. At the time of this writing, Danny attends university and helps teens with mental health problems. But he used to spend ten hours a day taking selfies. He'd scrutinize the photos for flaws and didn't post one until he felt it was perfect. He said, "I wanted to fit in and I thought the best way to do that was to be good looking." Eventually, he tried to commit suicide.

Today, more than ever, society is looking to itself for peace and inner security. We've put a man on the moon, flown planes at Mach 6, and grown body parts in petri dishes, but we've yet to engineer a way to satisfy the yearning of our hearts for fulfillment and well-being. Danny Bowman's two hundred selfies a day couldn't do it, the next generation iPhone won't do it, and whatever else man comes up with—to infinity and beyond—is certain to fail, too. Peace and security come only from having a relationship with God and being in His presence.

Jesus tells this to the church of Philadelphia in Revelation 3:12. Despite their trials and circumstances, God promises them a future of peace and security that would come from continually being in His presence. Jesus illustrates this by comparing them to *a pillar in the temple of my God.* The Greek word for "pillar" (*stylos*) refers to an extremely strong supporting beam. Because they are so hard to move, pillars represent security—in this case, security in the presence of God.

> Strabo, a Greek philosopher, called Philadelphia "a city full of earthquakes."

Because their Philadelphian lives *lacked* security, this illustration would have made a lot of sense. Philadelphia was located in the Lydian valley, where earthquakes were abundant. In 17 A.D., one of the most powerful earthquakes to that point in human history devastated Philadelphia. The damage was substantial. Tremors went on for years. These shocks made most of its citizens paranoid and ruined their sense of peace. They were always on edge, waiting for the next quake to destroy their buildings and homes. It wasn't unusual for people in Philadelphia to cower in fear and bolt from the city into open spaces when they felt the ground shaking.

GOD IS THE SOURCE OF TRUE PEACE

Yet God was assuring the Philadelphian believers that their peace did not come from this world. True peace comes from having a permanent fixture next to God. The whole city could be crumbling, but as long as the Philadelphians had their position near the throne, nothing could cause their peace to crumble.

When we spend our lives living in the presence of God, our peace comes from the security that God gives us. In fact, Jesus tells the Philadelphians that He does three things for those who live in His presence: He writes on them the *name* of God; He writes on them the *name* of God's city, the New Jerusalem; and He writes on them His new *name*. The Greek word for "name" (*onoma*) is repeated here three times. Repeating words is emphatic and is a signal to us of a major theme—in this case, ownership.

If God writes His name on us, it means we belong to Him. If He writes His city's name on us, it means that we are citizens of His kingdom. If Christ writes His new name on us, it means we are in Christ and share in His redemptive work. The name of the Lord is rock solid. (See Proverbs 18:10.) Nothing can demolish His property. Knowing this should give us comfort.

This week it is important to remember that your peace and security will never be found in what the world offers. Peace is supernatural and it is found in God. Lay down every relationship that you are looking to for acceptance, put away habits that you are using to provide satisfaction, and get away from vain imaginings that you hope will somehow bring fulfillment. Instead, seek the presence of God. You'll be at peace standing on that which can't be demolished.

PRAYER FOR THE WEEK

Dear Heavenly Father—
I recognize that peace and security come only from You. It is the great
desire of my heart to live in Your presence. The world cannot give me
anything to bring me assurance or fulfillment. Therefore, I lay down
everything that takes the place of Your presence in my life. Holy Spirit,
help me look to the Lord for total satisfaction. May nothing ever take
that place. In Jesus's name, amen!

ACTIVITY FOR THE WEEK

Spend time in the presence of God. Take the first and last half hour of
your day and spend it solely in God's presence. Turn on worship music if
you desire and set your affection on Christ. Tell him who is He to you and
what He means to your life. Let His presence fill your heart and give you
that sense of peace and security you need.

SCRIPTURES FOR THE WEEK

Isaiah 26:3	Philippians 4:6–7
Romans 8:6	Colossians 3:15
1 Corinthians 14:33	2 Thessalonians 3:16

PART VIII

THE CHURCH AT LAODICEA—STUDIES ON FAITHFULNESS

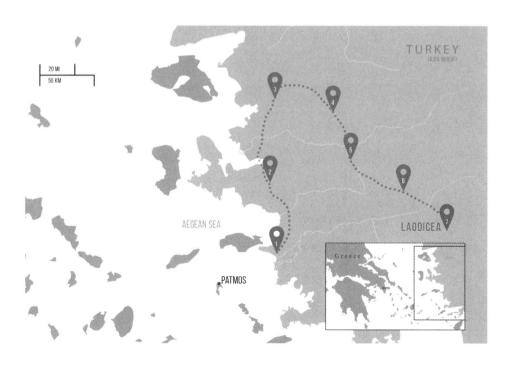

46

GOD DESERVES OUR COMMITMENT

And to the angel of the church in Laodicea write: The words of the Amen, the faithful and true witness, the beginning of God's creation. (Revelation 3:14)

Καὶ τῷ ἀγγέλῳ τῆς ἐν Λαοδικείᾳ ἐκκλησίας γράψον Τάδε λέγει ὁ ἀμήν, ὁ μάρτυς ὁ πιστὸς καὶ ἀληθινός, ἡ ἀρχὴ τῆς κτίσεως τοῦ θεοῦ. (ΑΠΟΚΑΛΥΨΙΣ ΙΩΑΝΝΟΥ 3:14)

Every guitar player I know says the same thing: "Les Pauls are the best." They're referring to a Gibson electric guitar, designed with the help of the late guitar innovator Les Paul. Les Pauls have been enabling guitarists to perform radical licks and riffs ever since the first one was sold in 1952.

Les Paul has quite the legacy. He's in the Rock and Roll Hall of Fame, the Songwriters Hall of Fame, the Grammy Hall of Fame, and the National Inventors Hall of Fame. Needless to say, he's an icon in the world of music and stringed instruments. Perhaps the most impressive thing about Les was his intense love and devotion to playing the guitar.

This became apparent in January 1948, when an accident in Oklahoma put his passion permanently at risk. The car driven by his future wife, Mary Ford, slid off the icy road and plummeted twenty feet into a frozen creek bed. She broke her pelvis; Les Paul broke six ribs, his nose, pelvis, and collarbone. Far worse, as far as he was concerned, his right arm was shattered so badly that one doctor suggested amputation.

Paul wasn't about to give up guitar playing. He asked the doctors to set his arm at a ninety-degree angle—and so they did. For the rest of his life, Paul couldn't raise is right arm *but* he could still remain faithful to what he loved the most: playing the guitar. That's commitment.

In Revelation 3:14, Jesus begins to speak to the Laodicean church about their faithfulness and commitment to Him. At one point, the Laodicean church had been healthy (see Colossians 4:16–17), but by the time Jesus addresses them, their faithfulness has more than just waned. They had become distracted by abundant wealth and luxurious living.

> "Laodicea" comes from the feminine Greek name "Laodice," from two Greek words: *laos* meaning "people" and *dike* meaning "rule." It means "rule of the people," referring to democracy. Prior to it being named Laodicea, it was called Diospolis and Rhoas. Antiochus of Syria named it Laodicea in honor of his sister, Laodice.

PRIDE IN WEALTH CAN DISTRACT US

At that time, Laodicea was one of the wealthiest cities in the world, a center for medicine, fashion, and finance. In fact, it was so well off that when it was hit by an earthquake in 61 A.D., it refused financial help from the Roman government. The city had enough resources of its own and insisted they could rebuild by themselves. This sort of pride in wealth and well-being had no doubt affected the Laodicean believers. The Lord wasn't happy about it. Prosperity is God's will (see 3 John 1:2), but it can turn into a distraction.

Those who are wealthy in this life have to be especially careful because wealth brings ease. And when people are on Easy Street, they often forget about their commitment to God. They can become too busy enjoying their money to serve the kingdom.

The way Jesus reveals Himself to the Laodicean church shows His displeasure toward their easy comfort and lack of commitment. He calls Himself two things: 1) the Amen; 2) the faithful and true witness (*ho Amēn, ho martys ho pistos kai alēthinos*). In the Greek, both "Amen" (*amēn*) and "witness" (*martys*) have the definite article (*ho*) in front of them.[48] *Ho* can be translated as *"the,"* which sets something into a class all by itself. It's like asking someone, "Hey, did you see *the* show?" They may reply, "What show?" Then you tell them, "*The* season finale." "*The*" refers to the most important show of all.

Here, Jesus was saying He is *"the* Amen" and *"the* faithful and true witness."[49] Not *an* Amen—*the* Amen; not *a* faithful witness—*the* faithful witness. His support and faithfulness to the Laodicean church was in a class by itself, unlike any other faithfulness in this world. His example of commitment is *the* epitome of what commitment is supposed to look like. This put the Laodicean church's lack of commitment into sharp contrast. After all Jesus had done for them, they had forgotten about Him because they were too busy enjoying their wealth.

God has been faithful and committed to you, there's no doubt about that. In fact, *nobody* has been as loyal to you as He is—including your employer, customers, friends, and family. In return, God deserves our hearts. Les Paul's story tells us that when we really love something, we find ways to stay committed instead of finding excuses why we can't. Do you think of ways to constantly demonstrate your commitment to God, or do you always accept life's excuses to sit out?

PRAYER FOR THE WEEK

Dear Heavenly Father—
You have been so faithful and committed to me. I could search the whole earth and never find someone who is as loyal to me as You. In re-

*turn, I give You my heart. Holy Spirit, put Your fire and passion in me.
Renew my commitment to God. May I take every chance I get to show
my loyalty to Jesus and serve His kingdom. In Jesus's name, amen!*

ACTIVITY FOR THE WEEK

Make a fresh commitment to God. Ask the Holy Spirit for His help,
then write a list of priorities that you plan to keep on a daily basis for the
next month. They should include prayer, giving, bible study, etc. If you are
married, decide on these with your spouse and hold each other to them.

SCRIPTURES FOR THE WEEK

1 King 8:61   Jeremiah 24:7

2 Kings 20:2–3   Jeremiah 29:13

1 Chronicles 28:9   Matthew 22:37

47

EXTREME FOR THE KINGDOM

I know your works: you are neither cold nor hot. Would that you were either cold or hot! So, because you are lukewarm, and neither hot nor cold, I will spit you out of my mouth.

(Revelation 3:15–16)

Οἶδά σου τὰ ἔργα ὅτι οὔτε ψυχρὸς εἶ οὔτε ζεστός. ὄφελον ψυχρὸς ἦς ἢ ζεστός. οὕτως ὅτι χλιαρὸς εἶ καὶ οὔτε ζεστὸς οὔτε ψυχρός, μέλλω σε ἐμέσαι ἐκ τοῦ στόματός μου.

(ΑΠΟΚΑΛΥΨΙΣ ΙΩΑΝΝΟΥ 3:15–16)

Do you drink your coffee hot or cold? Or both? My guess is you *don't* drink your coffee at room temperature. That's the worst. It's right up there with click bait, long voice mails, and the Facebook friend who "likes" every photo in your album.

I despise tepid coffee. In fact, I stocked up on cheap $7 coffee warmers and strategically positioned them in every room in my house. When I'm working or watching TV, these babies keep my java hot. When I drink my coffee on the deck, I attach one to an extension cord that connects to an outlet in the house. I know, I know—how inconvenient, right? But it's better than a mouthful of lousy, lukewarm coffee. Most people prefer their joe icy cold or near boiling hot...the same way God prefers His people.

> In biblical times, both cold wine and hot wine were normal, hospitable beverages to serve to guests. Snow was often used to chill wine; to heat wine, it was mixed with hot water. Wine was never served lukewarm because that was considered an insult to the guests, who could hold it against their host.

In Revelation 3:15–16, Jesus indicts the Laodicean church for being "lukewarm" (*chliaros*). The best way to describe what "lukewarm" means is to describe what it *doesn't* mean: cold or hot. "Cold" (*psychros*) often refers to "freezing" and "hot" (*zestos*) often refers to "boiling." Used together, they present the idea of being extreme. To be effective for the kingdom, we have to be extreme about the kingdom. Being lukewarm means uninvolved and passive. This attitude made the Laodicean church useless, like tepid coffee.

Being extreme for the kingdom means serving God's purposes with fervor and feeling. But the Laodiceans had lost this drive. They got used to Easy Street, switched on the cruise control, and were just getting by.

JESUS WANTS US TO BE EXTREME

Jesus didn't send His Holy Spirit into our lives and fill us with power so we could just get by. He wants us to rev the engine and put the pedal to the metal. In fact, extreme is our standard. Noah was extreme. Moses was extreme. David was extreme. Paul was extreme. Everyone in the book of Acts was extreme. Serving Christ isn't a Sunday drive. It's jumping a dirt bike across a spewing volcano and drag racing a 1957 Buick Special with fire breathing out of the mufflers. The Christian life is a thrilling life, full of passion and power. Those who neglect this have no profound effect.

The Laodiceans would have clearly understood that Jesus was calling them ineffective when he said they were neither cold nor hot, but lukewarm. Jesus was alluding to both their faith and their water system. Although wealthy, Laodicea had an awful water supply. Their neighbors fared differently. Just ten miles southwest of Laodicea was Colossae, which had an abundant supply of cold, refreshing water that was sweet to drink. Six miles north of Laodicea was Hierapolis, which had hot springs that provided sizzling water that was used for medicinal purposes and healing. Laodicea would pipe water in from around these regions. By the time the water got there, it was neither cold like the water of Colossae nor hot like the water of Hierapolis. It couldn't heal and it was repulsive to drink. Laodicea had become like its own water supply: stagnant, lukewarm, and good for nothing. They were no longer a place where people came to be healed and refreshed. They were a dispassionate, comfy social club of wealthy individuals who had no positive effect on the kingdom of God.

It's important for us to remember the Laodicean church when we are tempted to trade being extreme for Christ for an easy, comfortable Christianity…if such a thing exists. It's true many of us live in free and plentiful societies where life is more comfortable, but that comfort should never become a threat to the extremes that we will go to, to serve God. The kingdom of God should always remain our number one priority. We should always be passionate about it, even if we have to sacrifice our comforts.

This week, don't let your success thaw you out and don't let your comfort slow your simmer. Stay extreme for the Lord and step up when His kingdom calls. It may not always be fun, but it sure beats the taste of lukewarm.

PRAYER FOR THE WEEK

Dear Heavenly Father—
You've called me to be extreme. You desire my heart, my passion, my total involvement. May the things You've blessed me with never take the place of my willingness to go all out for Your kingdom. Holy Spirit, refresh my passion and restore my zeal. Rev my engine and get me

excited all over again about serving Your purposes. In Jesus's name, amen!

ACTIVITY FOR THE WEEK

Do what excites you. What do you think is the most exciting way to serve the kingdom? Witnessing? Praying for the sick? Interceding for the lost? Pick one and attempt to do it each day this week. When you are done, reflect. How has that rekindled your passion? How has it made you more effective? Has it broken you away from your comforts?

SCRIPTURES FOR THE WEEK

Psalm 42:1	Psalm 119:20
Psalm 63:1	Colossians 3:23
Psalm 84:2	Titus 2:14

48

WHEN YOU AREN'T AS WEALTHY AS YOU THINK

For you say, I am rich, I have prospered, and I need nothing, not realizing that you are wretched, pitiable, poor, blind, and naked. (Revelation 3:17)

ὅτι λέγεις ὅτι Πλούσιός εἰμι καὶ πεπλούτηκα καὶ οὐδὲν χρείαν ἔχω, καὶ οὐκ οἶδας ὅτι σὺ εἶ ὁ ταλαίπωρος καὶ ἐλεεινὸς καὶ πτωχὸς καὶ τυφλὸς καὶ γυμνός.

(ΑΠΟΚΑΛΥΨΙΣ ΙΩΑΝΝΟΥ 3:17)

Imagine blowing your life savings in just one night. Not sure about you, but I can't imagine it for long without freaking out. The mere thought of it makes my stomach crimp like a paper towel in the hands of a gorilla.

For one unfortunate man in southern China, the nightmare turned into a reality after he *thought* he won the lottery. The twenty-eight-year-old hopeful glitterati bought a lotto ticket and put it in a drawer for safekeeping. A week after the drawing, he decided to check the winning numbers. They seemed to match his; he thought he had won the jackpot of five million yuan ($788,000). Elated beyond belief, the young man took his friends out to a nightclub to celebrate. What a time they had! He spent his life savings of 5,000 yuan ($753) and put another 3,000 yuan ($451) on his credit card in just that one evening.

However, reality smacked the young man in the face when he woke the next morning. When he re-checked his ticket, it didn't have the winning numbers. Distraught and panicked, he called his girlfriend and told her he was going to commit suicide. The police had to come over and calm him down. He had thought he was rich when he wasn't—and it nearly ended fatally.

It's a dangerous thing to suppose we are doing better than we actually are. Jesus tells this to the church of Laodicea in Revelation 3:16. The Laodiceans had become quite impressed with themselves; they really had it goin' on. The money was piling up and they had access to the best medicine and fashions of the day. Sadly, they mistook their material wealth for their spiritual wealth. The wealthy often make this mistake. Christians, especially, need to make sure not to use their prosperity as evidence that God approves of their lifestyle. As seen in Laodicea, this is not always the case.

A "plutocracy" is a government that is run by the wealthy. This comes from the Greek words *plousios* ("rich") and *kratos* ("power"), meaning "the rich hold power." Therefore, a "plutocrat" is someone who uses their wealth to achieve political ambitions.

Jesus had been scrutinizing the attitude of the people of Laodicea and quotes them as saying "*I am rich, I have prospered, and I need nothing*" (*plousioskai eimi kai peploutēka kai ouden chreian cho*). The word order in the Greek is very strong and emphatic. It is another example of hysteron proteron. (See chapter 37; the writer takes the word that should be last and puts it first to emphasize it.) The word "rich" (*plousiokai*) is placed first. The phrase can literally be translated as "rich, I am" (*plousioskai eimi*). Riches, the people placed first. They were more impressed with wealth than they were with Jesus and their commitment was to money instead of serving the Lord.

JESUS EXPOSES OUR WEAKNESSES

We need to be careful not to assume that people who have money know some secret about having a relationship with the Lord that the rest of us are missing out on. Wealth, in and of itself, is no proof that a person has served the Lord with faithfulness of heart. Jesus exposes this when He says to them, *"You are wretched, pitiable, poor, blind, and naked."* These are personal, pointed criticisms. Remember, Laodicea was a center for medicine. They had one of the best eye ointments for treating damaged eyes. Yet, Jesus calls them blind. They were also a center for fashion and sold some of the finest black wool garments that money could buy. It was the Gucci of the day. Yet, Jesus says they are naked. They were a financial center and had great banks, yet Jesus calls them poor. Rich, high-society churchgoers were on the hot seat here, not because they were rich, but because riches held their hearts.

Who holds your heart? It's an easy thing to figure out. Does your relationship with the Lord center only around wealth? Is it the essence of what you use to relate to God? Do all your spiritual activities revolve around it? Are *all* of your podcasts about acquiring wealth "the kingdom way"? Are the only Bible verses you highlight ones about money? If yes, while I commend you for reading and listening to the Word, there's an imbalance somewhere. Sure, it's good to study wealth from God's Word, but if that's *all* you study, it could be very telling about what ultimately you want from God.

The same God who tells us how to handle our money and leads us into blessing has also told us to take up our crosses to follow Him. (See Matthew 16:24–26.) If we aren't willing to accept this part of the message as fervently as the parts about money, then it's certain we are committed to money above the Lord—and we aren't as wealthy as we think.

PRAYER FOR THE WEEK

Dear Heavenly Father—
Above money and wealth, my heart is committed to You. I know that
it is Your desire for me to be prosperous, but may my prosperity never
take Your place. Holy Spirit, may I keep greed and selfish ambitions
out of my life. May my possessions and position never be what I use to
determine how close I am with You. I embrace the cross You have told
me to carry and will carry it no matter what it costs. In Jesus's name,
amen!

ACTIVITY FOR THE WEEK

Take inventory. Consider your material possessions. Is there anything more important to you than the Lord? Your car, home, salary, clothes? If yes, ask the Holy Spirit to search your heart. Reflect. How does the Lord feel about the place it has in your life? Would God bless you even more if you were able to put Him above it?

SCRIPTURES FOR THE WEEK

Psalm 62:10	Philippians 4:11–13
Matthew 6:19–20	1 Timothy 6:6–10
2 Corinthians 9:8	Hebrews 13:5

49

A BRAND YOU CAN TRUST

I counsel you to buy from me gold refined by fire, so that you may be rich, and white garments so that you may clothe yourself and the shame of your nakedness may not be seen, and salve to anoint your eyes, so that you may see. (Revelation 3:18)

συμβουλεύω σοι ἀγοράσαι παρ' ἐμοῦ χρυσίον πεπυρωμένον ἐκ πυρὸς ἵνα πλουτήσῃς, καὶ ἱμάτια λευκὰ ἵνα περιβάλῃ καὶ μὴ φανερωθῇ ἡ αἰσχύνη τῆς γυμνότητός σου, καὶ κολλ[ο]ύριον ἐγχρῖσαι τοὺς ὀφθαλμούς σου ἵνα βλέπῃς. (ΑΠΟΚΑΛΥΨΙΣ ΙΩΑΝΝΟΥ 3:18)

You never know whom you're buying from. That's especially true today. We've all heard Craigslist horror stories that make us think twice before picking up that coffee table that will go nicely with our couch. But if we're talking about shady salespeople, let's go way back to 1925. Victor Lustig, "the smoothest con man who ever lived," was in Paris, France, and was selling the Eiffel Tower. It's considered one of the greatest con jobs of all time.

One day, Lustig read in the newspaper that the French government was having a difficult time maintaining the Eiffel Tower and paying the costs of upkeep, so they considered tearing it down. Lustig took advantage of this news. He pretended to be a French government official and forged stationery that he used to send invitations to the largest scrap-metal dealers in France. He had them meet him at an upscale Parisian hotel and told them the government was having him take bids on the 7,000 tons of metal. To top off the con, Lustig rented limos and gave the potential buyers tours of the tower.

Lustig noticed that one of the bidders seemed eager to make a name for himself. His ambition made him a perfect target. So Lustig offered him a bribe: in exchange for $70,000 in cash, Lustig would make sure this man's company got the bid. The man bit and in an hour, Lustig had the cash and was on a train to Austria. The bidder eventually realized he had been conned, but was so embarrassed, he never reported the crime. Lustig got away with it scot-free. The bidder, unfortunately, looked for wealth and fame from the wrong source.

> The Greek verb "to buy" is agorazō. This word comes from *agora*, meaning "market" or "marketplace." In ancient Greece, the *agora* was the customary place for trade and commerce.

If we look to sources that are not dependable, we will end up bankrupt and shamed. True spiritual wealth has only one genuine source: Jesus. All other sources are cons and schemes; they can't deliver what they promise. Jesus tells this to the Laodicean church in Revelation 3:18. He says, "*I counsel you to buy from me*" (*symbouleuō soi agorasai par' emou*). The manner of this statement in the Greek makes it emphatic.[50] Jesus is saying, "Buy *from Me!*" The Lord is really stressing, "Don't go buying from anyone or anything else, no matter how good it might look. Buy from me alone!" Jesus is the *only* reliable source of spiritual welfare. Therefore, our spiritual well-being is reliant on our loyalty to Christ. So, we must develop a brand loyalty toward Him.

When customers are loyal to a brand, they buy it over and over again. I have a few of these loyalties myself. For instance, I buy the same kind of coffee every time I go shopping. The coffee section in my grocery store has waves of colorful packages of roasts from all over the world, but I surf through it until I find *my* blonde roast and then I'm gone.

WE NEED TO BE LOYAL TO JESUS

Yet, the Laodiceans didn't have this same loyalty to Christ. They were divided on what could actually bring them the satisfaction they wanted and chose materialism rather than Jesus. Sadly, there are people in the church today who do this all too often. Instead of seeking Christ for peace, they end up going to a Zen class to try Eastern meditation. Instead of looking to God's Word for wisdom, they mess with philosophies that inspire doubt toward everything God has said. If they're lonely, instead of seeking God and building healthy friendships with His people, they seek out romance the way the world says it should be done. All of these people will be disappointed more than the man who thought he was buying the Eiffel Tower.

God's Word tells us that we don't need any other source besides Him. He tells us that we are complete in Christ. (See Colossians 2:10.) Jesus is a one-stop shop who stocks the finest gifts for you. You are certain to find exactly what you are looking for. No need to go anywhere else—His products won't let you down or put you to shame. On the contrary, they will make you a satisfied customer, over and over again. Stick to your brand, stick to Jesus—He's a God you can trust.

PRAYER FOR THE WEEK

Dear Heavenly Father—
You are the genuine source of all that is good, and I know that what You offer will never disappoint. Therefore, I declare, I will always stay loyal to You. I am not interested in looking elsewhere to things that are certain to disappoint. Holy Spirit, help me to access the riches of all that God has to offer me in Christ. All of my life, I will speak about how satisfied I am in You, Lord. In Jesus's name, amen!

ACTIVITY FOR THE WEEK

Make God's Word your favorite brand. In your prayer journal, come up with a logo and a slogan that describes the satisfying delight that serving Jesus brings. Use it to remind yourself why you serve the Lord faithfully each day.

SCRIPTURES FOR THE WEEK

Psalm 16:5–6	John 15:1–8
Psalm 23:5–6	Philippians 4:19–20
John 1:16	Colossians 2:10

50

DON'T CRY
ABOUT CORRECTION

Those whom I love, I reprove and discipline, so be zealous and repent. (Revelation 3:19)

ἐγὼ ὅσους ἐὰν φιλῶ ἐλέγχω καὶ παιδεύω. ζήλευε οὖν καὶ μετανόησον. (ΑΠΟΚΑΛΥΨΙΣ ΙΩΑΝΝΟΥ 3:19)

When you're six years old, nothing is worse than a spanking from dad. Sometimes I can *still* feel the scorching bite of my dad's paddle doing the waltz upon my buttocks. My brain has made sure I never forget because the nerves in my body never want to feel that shocking agony again. *Anything but the paddle!*

I had my fair share of spankings growing up, but my most memorable one happened because I refused to obey my parents and wear my winter hat during recess at school. They gave me specific instructions to put it on because they didn't want me getting sick. I had disobeyed once already. They warned me another infraction would result in "discipline." But, hey, when you're in the first grade, it's not cool to wear a dopey-looking hat on the playground. I needed some chest hairs. And wearing a clumsy beany my grandmother knit wasn't going to help me grow them. Well, it just so happened my mother came to the school one day and saw me outside without it on. On the way home, I asked her a million times, "Are you going to tell dad?" and she just kept on nodding. *GULP.*

My dad came home and sent me to my room. Then, he ate his whole dinner while I waited in suspense. I thought, *how can he actually eat at a time like this?* Finally, he came upstairs and grilled my backside. What's funny is, though my rear was searing like ahi tuna, the pain I felt inside for letting my parents down hurt the most. To my relief, my dad came back into my room ten minutes later and gave me a hug. Tears slopped down my face like water in a cup carried by a wobbly three-year-old. My dad didn't have to say anything; I knew he loved me and I knew why he did it: he didn't want either of us to go through the pain of my being sick. To this day, I still wear my hat in the bitter cold. His love and correction helped me form a new healthy habit.

> "Philosophy" comes from *philos* ("love") and *sophia* ("wisdom"). It literally means the "love of wisdom." A person who studies philosophy is giving special interest and attention to wisdom.

The purpose of discipline is not to ruin us. Quite the opposite. It's a demonstration of love meant to set us on a new and better course for our lives. It's a caring redirection of actions and habits that result in our victory and success. This is what Jesus tells the Laodiceans. He explains that the correction He just gave them was because He loves (*phileō*) them. *Phileō* means, "to give someone special attention and special interest; special affection." It was used to describe the way people love their country, spouses, and children. It's faithful, committed, and abhors the idea of something bad happening to the thing it's connected to. Think of how you feel when something threatens your country and family. That's *phileō*. Despite the Laodiceans' unfaithfulness to Jesus, He was committed to their well-being.

JESUS OFFERS LOVING CORRECTION

Because Jesus wanted the best for the Laodiceans, He hoped that His loving correction would make them live differently. He wanted them to take advantage of it so He says, "be zealous" (*zēleue*). This is found in a manner which means that Jesus wanted no less than a strong and continuous effort on the Laodiceans' part, demanding a fresh commitment with new habits.[51] They were to make the most of His correction and use it as an opportunity to grow.

The whole point of correction is to make us more mature. God's doesn't do it because He wants to make us feel like an earthworm on the sidewalk after a rain. He's not into torture. He's more interested in seeing us get our priorities straight. If that doesn't happen, then the correction hasn't worked, no matter how bad it stings. When God corrects you, don't get too hung up on how it feels. Most of that comes from a damaged sense of pride anyway. Make the most of it and decide how you are going to respond. Do you have a new course of action? What will your new habits look like? What new choices is God leading you to make?

Mature Christians see correction as an opportunity. They welcome it. They receive it. They rejoice over it. It is God's grace in their life that will bolster fresh engagement with Him and a chance to better serve Him. If God corrects you this week, don't sulk. Seize the moment to revise your priorities so you can become even more faithful to God. You never know what godly habits God's correction might produce in your life. Whatever it may be, it will help you serve the Lord for a lifetime to come. Aren't you thankful that the Lord loves us…and corrects us?

PRAYER FOR THE WEEK

Dear Heavenly Father—
I am not running from Your correction. In fact, I see it as a great opportunity. It is Your love and grace entering my life in an effort to help me become closer to You. Sure, it might sting. But the pain of Your

correction doesn't compare to the joy that comes from walking hand-in-hand with You. I receive Your correction; I welcome it; I rejoice that You love me enough to bring it into my life. You are that interested in me. In Jesus's name, amen!

ACTIVITY FOR THE WEEK

Consider some of the healthy habits you have in your life. Did any of these come (or have they been strengthened) because God corrected you at some point in your walk with Him? What role do these habits play in helping you walk close to the Lord? How would you fare without them?

SCRIPTURES FOR THE WEEK

2 Samuel 7:14–15

Job 5:17

Psalm 119:75

Proverbs 3:11

Proverbs 15:12

1 Corinthians 11:32

51

JESUS,
THE DOOR KNOCKER

Behold, I stand at the door and knock. If anyone hears my voice and opens the door, I will come in to him and eat with him, and he with me. (Revelation 3:20)

ἰδοὺ ἕστηκα ἐπὶ τὴν θύραν καὶ κρούω. ἐάν τις ἀκούσῃ τῆς φωνῆς μου καὶ ἀνοίξῃ τὴν θύραν, [καὶ] εἰσελεύσομαι πρὸς αὐτὸν καὶ δειπνήσω μετ᾽ αὐτοῦ καὶ αὐτὸς μετ᾽ ἐμοῦ.
(ΑΠΟΚΑΛΥΨΙΣ ΙΩΑΝΝΟΥ 3:20)

When people knock on my door, I'm not likely to answer. I prefer hiding out. If I want something, I'll buy it on Amazon—no need for someone to sell it to me on the porch. But there are times when a knock at the door has been known to change someone's life.

In 2014, Stephanie Headley of Ottawa, Canada, was dying. She had systemic scleroderma, an autoimmune disease that attacks the body. Her skin was tightening and her organs were beginning to harden. There was a stem cell treatment that could possibly save her life. But it cost $125,000. She didn't have the money.

One day, Stephanie was at home and there was a knock at her door. It wasn't a pesky salesman or a neighbor wanting to borrow some sugar. It was a mystery man wearing a hat, sunglasses, and a jacket that was zipped up all the way in order to hide his identity. He said nothing. He just handed Stephanie an envelope, smiled, and walked away. When Stephanie opened the envelope, she began to weep. Inside was a check for $128,000. Stephanie had another chance at life because of the knock at her door. She lived for four more years before she succumbed to the disease.

JESUS WON'T GIVE UP ON US

In Revelation 3:20, the Laodiceans had a surprise visitor of their own, knocking at their door. Jesus had come to make the unfaithful church an offer they wouldn't be able to refuse: a second chance with Him. He tells them, *"Behold, I stand at the door and knock"* (*idou hestēka epi tēn thyran kai krouō*). It could technically be translated, "I have stood at your door and I remain here standing."[52] It gives us a picture of a persistent person who keeps knocking, who doesn't want to leave because he has something important for those inside, like the mystery man who handed Stephanie the money she needed.

Next, we find the word "knock" (*krouō*) in the present tense. This implies an ongoing knocking. Jesus isn't shy about His offer. He's bold and is trying to get their attention by knocking, knocking, and knocking some more. This is unlike how I used to be when I'd to go door-to-door as a youth, collecting cans. Here in Michigan, we get ten cents for every aluminum can we return to the store. For fundraisers, we would collect them from neighbors. I was shy, however. I'd barely knock, wait fifteen seconds, and then say, "See, they aren't home. Let's go." Jesus was quite the opposite. He camped out on the Laodiceans' porch and He was a-knockin'.

It's interesting how interested Jesus is in the Laodiceans despite how disinterested and uncommitted they had been toward Jesus. This just shows that Jesus is the ultimate picture of God's love. He doesn't treat us the way we treat Him. He was committed to us before we were ever committed to Him. (See Romans 5:8.) For this, He will forever be called Faithful and True. (See Revelation 19:11.)

> Dinner in Greco-Roman days would have included eggs, olives, fish, various kinds of cheese, fruits and vegetables, and bread that was to be dipped into wine and olive oil. Meats were more common among the wealthy.

Jesus tells the Laodiceans what He wants, *"I will come in to him and eat with him, and he with me."* The Greek word here "eat" (deipneō) refers to eating dinner. Jesus doesn't just want to have a snack with the Laodiceans. He wants to have *dinner* with them. This was a big deal. In Greco Roman days, there were three meals: Breakfast (*akratisma*), lunch (*ariston*), and dinner (*deipnon*). Breakfast was a piece of bread and wine; lunch was usually just a light snack eaten on the go. But dinner was the largest meal of the day and a time of close fellowship, enjoyment, and affection. It was eaten with people you loved, cared about, and enjoyed being around—just as it is today.

Christ's invitation to dinner was metaphorical: He wanted to renew His relationship with the Laodiceans. He wanted to bury the hatchet, put the past in the past, and restore what they had. This meant having an intimate relationship with Christ *now* and also sharing in Christ's messianic kingdom when He returns. What a generous offer to a church that didn't deserve it.

This week, it's important to know that the glue that holds our relationship with Christ together is ultimately *His* commitment and faithfulness to *us*. Think of all the times you've done Him wrong, disobeyed, and have been slow to listen or slow to speak. Yet our faithful Lord always comes back to the door and stands there knocking until we take Him up on His offer to become close again. If you have let Him down, don't worry about it any longer. Stop getting down on yourself. Instead, go answer the knock at the door. Jesus wants to give you another chance—again. He wants to have dinner with you.

PRAYER FOR THE WEEK

Dear Heavenly Father—
Thank You that You are faithful and true. All of my life, You have been
the one who seeks me and draws me into fellowship with You. Lord
Jesus, I honor Your devotion to me. Thank You for being interested in
our relationship even when I acted indifferent. I love You and I open
my heart to You today. Please come in and dine with me. In Jesus's
name, amen!

ACTIVITY FOR THE WEEK

Have dinner with Jesus. This week, if you are eating alone, invite Jesus
to dine with you. First, welcome His presence. Tell Him you want to enjoy
His company and you would be honored to have Him as your guest. As you
eat, consider His goodness and loyalty to you. Allow your heart to worship
Him for creating the beautiful fellowship that you have together.

SCRIPTURES FOR THE WEEK

Ezekiel 34:11–12

Psalm 119:176

Luke 12:37

Luke 19:10

John 10:3–5

John 21:1–19

52

TESTED TO TAKE
THE THRONE

---

*The one who conquers, I will grant him to sit with me on my
throne, as I also conquered and sat down with my Father on his
throne.* (Revelation 3:21)

ὁ νικῶν δώσω αὐτῷ καθίσαι μετ' ἐμοῦ ἐν τῷ θρόνῳ μου,
ὡς κἀγὼ ἐνίκησα καὶ ἐκάθισα μετὰ τοῦ πατρός μου ἐν τῷ
θρόνῳ αὐτοῦ. (ΑΠΟΚΑΛΥΨΙΣ ΙΩΑΝΝΟΥ 3:21)

There's no feeling quite as helpless as losing your wallet in a public place.
It's frightening to think of your cash, credit cards, and personal information in the hands of a total stranger, perhaps even a malevolent stranger.
I've been there a few times in my life and it's despairing. It might be even
more miserable when a celebrity loses their wallet. It's highly possible that

someone could not only take all of their cash, but also take advantage of their private information.

Chris Hemsworth—the actor who portrays Thor in the *Avengers* movies—may have felt this way when he accidentally left his wallet at a restaurant.

Fortunately for Hemsworth, a young man with integrity found it and returned it to him in the mail without taking a buck. However, the teen did have one request. Hemsworth was going to be on *The Ellen DeGeneres Show* and the teen's mother wanted to know if they could get tickets.

Not only did they get tickets, but the actor wanted to repay the young man's honesty in an even greater way. Hemsworth gave the teen all of the money that had been in the wallet, plus some extra, and an additional $10,000 from *Shutterfly,* the image publishing company. Hemsworth shared his wealth and influence with the young man because he was a loyal fan who didn't betray him.

In Revelation 2:21, Jesus tells the church in Laodicea that He will openly reward all those who are loyal to Him. He says, *"I will grant him to sit on my throne with me."* Jesus is talking about a future rule with Him in His millennial reign (see Revelation 20:2–7) and beyond. A throne represents power, influence, and authority. Jesus plans to share this with those who overcome sin and stay faithful to Him during the perilous times in our world.

> Thrones for two or more were common in the Greco-Roman world. An example of this is found on ancient Greek art from 500 B.C. portraying Zeus and Hera on a double throne, reigning together.

The interesting thing is that Jesus mentions other people sitting on His throne with Him. Often, people wonder how more than one person can sit on a throne. In our minds, a throne is a seat where a single monarch rules. However, the Greek word "throne" (*thronos*) implies something different. In those times, thrones often looked more like a couch than a single seat. They were broad and wide, built for two or more, resembling a sofa or bench. Jesus isn't planning to rule alone. He wants His loyal people to take a seat on the throne beside Him to help Him govern.

It is a tremendous thing to consider that Jesus will entrust us with the responsibility to rule with Him. Some of us have a hard time comprehending that the company we work for lets us operate one of its machines, let alone trying to grasp that God plans to entrust us with eternal responsibility over His vast kingdom. But God knows that when that time comes, we will be ready. That's because this life is preparation for the next. All of the tests, difficulties, temptations, and challenges are proving our hearts to determine whether we will be trustworthy to take a position with Christ upon His throne.

ALL OF LIFE'S TESTS PREPARE US

With this in mind, you should never look at a test in your life as insignificant and inconsequential. These things come to try our hearts and test our loyalty. Is it toward ourselves and the world, or is it toward Jesus Christ and His kingdom? This life is a series of quizzes and tests leading up to the final exam. We are being stretched to the limit to see what we are made of. During these times, God takes His measurements and keeps them in mind as He considers us for our position next to Him. Thankfully, He has given to us the grace and mercy we need for each challenge so that we can assume the place next to Him that He is preparing for us.

This week, remember that you are being prepared for the throne. Will you allow the persecutions from your family to grind your gears? Will you allow temptations that are pleasing to the flesh bend your metal? Will you let cultural lies put you out of commission? Or will you rise to the occasion and stay faithful to the one who is called Faithful and True? Just remember, if you do: He has a place for you next to Him in eternity and He plans to share all of His goodness with you.

PRAYER FOR THE WEEK

Dear Heavenly Father—
I thank You and I praise You that You have called me to rule and reign
with You. You fully intend to share Your power and authority with me

in the age to come. This life is just preparation for Your throne. It is humbling to think about and to consider, and for this I am eternally thankful. Holy Spirit, help me to pass each test in life. Give me the grace I need to use every obstacle as an opportunity to prove faithful to You. I want to be Your joy and delight. In Jesus's name, amen!

ACTIVITY FOR THE WEEK

Prepare yourself to rule with Christ on His throne in eternity by using the authority He has given in this life to rule over the things He has placed under your feet. Make a list of every hindering thing that is troubling your life. Place a Scripture next to each thing that shows you have the victory over it. Now, stomp on that paper and declare that Christ has given you full authority over the challenges in this life.

SCRIPTURES FOR THE WEEK

Daniel 7:21–22, 27	2 Timothy 2:12
Romans 5:17	1 Peter 4:13
Ephesians 2:6	Revelation 20:4–6

LAST WORDS

As generations cycle and the topography of the culture changes, the message of Christ to the seven churches remains the same. It serves as anchor of truth that we can tie our lives to so we aren't swept away by tsunamis of subjectivity and sin.

I'm not sure what the culture will come up with next or what the "experts" will soon "discover." But I can tell you that there are seven messages that give us the mandate to overcome whatever that might be. And we will.

Thank God for His Word and thank God for His Holy Spirit. May we continue to trust in the seven letters from Jesus.

ABOUT THE AUTHOR

The Rev. Chris Palmer is the founder and pastor of Light of Today Church in Novi, Michigan, and founder of Chris Palmer Ministries. He is host of the popular podcast, *Greek for the Week*, seen on several Internet platforms.

Chris began in full-time ministry in 2006 and began to preach internationally in 2009, helping many congregations grow, flourish, and expand. His desire for missions is to train and educate pastors, encourage congregations, support the vision of local church, and show the love of God to the culture. He has done this successfully for a decade in over forty nations of the world in Europe, Africa, South America, Asia, and the Caribbean, working with both traditional churches and the underground and persecuted church.

Chris earned a B.A. in Pastoral Studies from North Central University and an M.A. in Exegetical Theology, magna cum laude, from Moody Theological Seminary. He is a sought-after Greek scholar for his ability to make God's Word come alive from the Greek in a unique way. Chris is often invited to present Greek and hermeneutics workshops at Bible and ministry schools. He recently began working on his Ph.D. at the University of Wales, Bangor, in the area of Johannine literature, particularly the book of Revelation.

His previous books include the self-published *Living as a Spirit: Hearing the Voice of God on Purpose, The 85 Questions You Ask When You Begin a Relationship with God, The Believer's Journey,* and *Escaping the Haunting Past: A Handbook for Deliverance.*

BIBLIOGRAPHY

"2003 Blackout hits Northeast United States." History.com (www.history.com/this-day-in-history/blackout-hits-northeast-united-states, accessed July 5, 2018).

"Chris Hemsworth surprises teenager who returned his lost wallet." Hellomagazine.com (us.hellomagazine.com/celebrities/2016041830963/chris-hemsworth-surprises-young-boy-who-returned-his-wallet, accessed July 1, 2018).

"Jesus is my homeboy." Jesusismyhomeboy.com (www.jesusismyhomeboy.com/the-story, accessed July 6, 2018).

"Wolverine: Chasing the Phantom." PBS.org (www.pbs.org/wnet/nature/wolverine-chasing-the-phantom-wolverine-facts/6049, accessed June 24, 2018).

Abbott, Karen. "The 1904 Olympic Marathon May Have Been the Strangest Ever." Smihtsonianmag.org (www.smithsonianmag.com/history/the-1904-olympic-marathon-may-have-been-the-strangest-ever-14910747, accessed June 17, 2018).

Aland, Barbara, Kurt Aland, Johannes Karavidopoulos, Carlo M. Martini, and Bruce M. Metzger, eds. *The Greek New Testament*. Fifth Revised Edition. Stuttgart, Germany: Deutsche Bibelgesellschaft, 2014.

Alimurung, Gendy. "The Man Who Smelled Too Much." Laweekly.com (www.laweekly.com/news/the-man-who-smelled-too-much-2612005, accessed July 2, 2018).

Associated Press. "Keeping Promise, man listens to Cubs win at Dad's grave site." Kwese.espn.com (kwese.espn.com/mlb/story/_/id/17963668/ keeping-promise-man-listens-chicago-cubs-win-dad-gravesite, accessed June 22, 2018).

Aune, David E. *Revelation 1–5*. Vol. 52A. Word Biblical Commentary. Dallas: Word, Incorporated, 1998.

Barclay, William. *The Revelation of John*. 3rd ed. fully rev. and updated. Vol. 1. The New Daily Study Bible. Louisville, KY; London: Westminster John Knox Press, 2004.

Beale, G. K. *The Book of Revelation: A Commentary on the Greek Text*. New International Greek Testament Commentary. Grand Rapids, MI; Carlisle, Cumbria: W.B. Eerdmans; Paternoster Press, 1999.

Dion, Don. "Warren Buffett Steps Up and Helps His Shareholders With Airbnb." Seekingalpha.com (seekingalpha.com/article/2186073-warren-buffett-steps-up-and-helps-his-shareholders-with-airbnb, accessed July 9, 2018).

Gan, Nectar. "Chinese man blows savings celebrating US$780,000 lottery win…then finds out he was mistaken." SCMP.Com (www.scmp.com/ news/china/society/article/2134413/chinese-man-suicidal-after-mistakenly-thinking-hed-won-lottery, accessed June 25, 2018).

Gilbertson, Joan. "Frozen Boy: 10 Years After Being Brought Back to Life." Minnesota.CBSlocal.com (minnesota.cbslocal.com/2011/02/03/frozen-boy-10-years-after-being-brought-back-to-life, accessed July 1, 2018).

Griffiths, Mark D. Ph.D. "Obsessive Selfie-Taking. Psychologytoday.com (www.psychologytoday.com/us/ blog/in-excess/201801/obsessive-selfie-taking, accessed June 21, 2018).

Harlow, Poppy and David Goldman. "Warren Buffett endorses Airbnb." Cnn.money.com (money.cnn.com/2014/04/09/technology/social/buffett-airbnb/index.html, accessed July 9, 2018).

Hort, F. J. A. *The Apocalypse of St. John 1–3: The Greek Text with Introduction, Commentary, and Additional Notes*. London: Macmillan and Co., 1908.

Howell, Elizabeth. "Opportunity: Longest-Running Mars Rover." Space. com (www.space.com/18289-opportunity-rover.html, accessed July 7, 2018).

Howerton, Jason. "A Stranger Knocked on Her Door and, Without Saying a Word, Handed Her a Life Changing Envelope That Made Her 'Collapse.'" Theblaze.com (www.theblaze.com/news/2014/07/16/a-stranger-knocked-on-her-door-and-without-saying-a-word-handed-her-a-life-changing-envelope-that-made-her-to-collapse, July 10, 2018).

Isaac, Brad. "Jerry Seinfeld's Productivity Secret." Lifehacker.com (life-hacker.com/281626/jerry-seinfelds-productivity-secret, accessed July 4, 2018).

Johnson, Ben. "The Great Fire of London." Historic-UK.com (www.historic-uk.com/HistoryUK/ HistoryofEngland/The-Great-Fire-of-London, accessed June 22, 2018).

King, Gilbert. "The Smoothest Con Man That Ever Lived." Smithsonianmag.com (www.smithsonianmag.com/history/the-smoothest-con-man-that-ever-lived-29861908, accessed June 19, 2018).

Koester, Craig. *Revelation*. The Anchor Yale Bible Commentaries. New Haven, CT: Yale University Press, 2014.

Lawrence, Robb. *The Early Years of the Les Paul Legacy, 1915-1963*. (New York, NY: Hal Leonard Books, 2008), 26.

MacDowell, Douglas M. *The Law in Classical Athens*. Ithaca, NY: Cornell University Press, 1978.

McIlhaney Jr, Joe S. and Freda McKissic Bush. *Hooked: New Science on How Casual Sex is Affecting Our Children*. Chicago, IL: Northfield Publishing, 2008.

Morales, Tatiana. "An Orphan's Dream Lands on Mars." CBSNews.com (www.cbsnews.com/news/an-orphans-dream-lands-on-mars, accessed July 3, 2018).

Morris, Leon. *Revelation: An Introduction and Commentary*. Vol. 20. Tyndale New Testament Commentaries. Downers Grove, IL: InterVarsity Press, 1987.

Mounce, Robert H. *The Book of Revelation*. The New International Commentary on the New Testament. Grand Rapids, MI: Wm. B. Eerdmans Publishing Co., 1997.

Nolte, Carl. "The Great Quake: 1906-2006 / Rising from the ashes." SFGate.com (www.sfgate.com/news/article/The-Great-Quake-1906-2006-Rising-from-the-ashes-2537103.php, accessed June 28, 2018).

Shah, Bela. "Addicted to selfies: I take 200 snaps a day." BBC.com (www.bbc.com/news/newsbeat-43197018, accessed June 19, 2018).

Shavin, Naomi.. "The Ancient History of Cheating in the Olympics." Smithsonianmag.com (www.smithsonianmag.com/history/ancient-history-cheating-olympics-180960003, accessed June 15, 2018).

Simcox, William Henry. *The Revelation of S. John the Divine*. Cambridge Greek Testament for Schools and Colleges. Cambridge: Cambridge University Press, 1893.

Smalley, Stephen S. *The Revelation to John: A Commentary on the Greek Text of the Apocalypse*. London: SPCK, 2005.

Stein, James. "The Chandrasekhar Limit: The Threshold that Makes Life Possible." PBS.org (www.pbs.org/wgbh/nova/article/the-chandrasekhar-limit-the-threshold-that-makes-life-possible, accessed June 23, 2018).

Swete, Henry Barclay, ed. *The Apocalypse of St. John*. 2d. ed. Classic Commentaries on the Greek New Testament. New York: The Macmillan Company, 1906.

The Holy Bible: English Standard Version. Wheaton: Standard Bible Society, 2016.

Thomas, Robert L. *Revelation 1-7: An Exegetical Commentary*. Chicago: Moody Publishers, 1992.

Trail, Ronald. *An Exegetical Summary of Revelation 1–11*. 2nd ed. Dallas, TX: SIL International, 2008.

Trench, Richard Chenevix. *Commentary on the Epistles to the Seven Churches in Asia*. Fourth Edition, Revised. London: Kegan Paul, Trench, & Co., 1886.

ENDNOTES

1. There is an ongoing discussion among scholars about whether the messages in Revelation 2–3 circulated as one letter or if they were seven separate letters. Be as it may, the messages were written like separate letters. For that reason, we may refer to them as seven separate letters, even if it circulated as one letter.

2. John should've placed "him who is" (*ho ōn*) in the genitive case but, instead, he puts it in the nominative case.

3. In Exodus, *ho ōn* is found correctly in the nominative case. To use it correctly in Revelation 1:4, John would have needed to switch it into the genitive case. But making the case change would cause the phrase to lose its significance.

4. This is the genitive case. The genitive case would imply to take hold "of" something (in part).

5. This is the accusative case.

6. Some menorahs have seven branches, known as a *candelabra*. There is a famous one found outside near the Israeli Knesset. Other menorahs have nine branches, known as a *Chanukiyyah*, which are used only during Chanukah to commemorate the Maccabees' victory over the Greco/Syrians in 165 B.C.

7. The present tense (functioning progressively).

8. *Oida is* in the perfect tense.

9. *Mnēmoneuō* is in the present tense (functioning progressively).

10. *Metanoeō* is in the aorist tense.

11. *Akouō* is the aorist tense (functioning constatively) and in the imperative mood (giving a command).

12. *Tō nikōnti* forms a present participle (which functions continuously).

13. *America's Got Talent*. Directed by Russell Norman. NBC, 2006–present.

14. *Egeneto* is in the aorist tense (functioning constatively).

15. *Ezēsen* in the aorist tense (functioning ingressively).

16 *Ouk* (not) is a negative particle that always denies an alleged fact.

17. *Mēden* (from *mēdeis*) is the strongest negative particle that can be used to negate. It is also connected to fear (*phobou*) which is in the imperative mood. This adds additional strength and urgency to the statement.

18. *Hēmerōn* is found in the genitive case and is functioning temporally. This means that the Smyrnaean's suffering was limited. In this case, to ten days.

19. "Be" (*ginou*) is in the present tense and in the imperative mood. Present imperatives can mean urgent, continued action.

20. *Forrest Gump*, directed by Robert Zemeckis (1994; Paramount Pictures).

21. Life (*tēs zōēs*) is in the genitive case functioning appositionally. This means that "life" explains what the crown (*ton stephanon*) is.

22. Here "Satan" (*tou Satana*) is in the genitive case and is functioning subjectively. This means that Satan was taking action from his throne.

23. *Ērnēsō* is found in the aorist tense and in the indicative mood.

24. This is suggested by the progressive present tense that *echeis* is found in here.

25. The word "mouth" (stomatos) is found in the genitive case and is functioning descriptively. It means that "mouth" is describing "sword."

26. *Oun* is an inferential conjunction. It introduces a concluding remark.

27. *The Passion of the Christ*, directed by Mel Gibson (2004; Newmarket Films).

28. www.jesusismyhomeboy.com.

29. The word "God" (*theou*) here is found in the genitive case and is being used relationally.

30. *Echōn* is a nominative participle in apposition. *Echōn* is working to clarify something about Jesus.

31. The word "exceed" (*pleiona*) is an adjective and means "great in number; great in size, mighty; valuable." Here, "exceed" (*pleiona*) is functioning as a comparative adjective.

32. *Apheis* is found in the present tense and active voice.

33. Joe McIlhaney, Freda McKissic Bush, *Hooked: New Science on How Casual Sex Is Affecting Our Children* (Chicago: Northfield Publishing, 2008).

34. *Edōka* is found in the aorist tense functioning constatively.

35. Wishes (*thelei*) is found in the present tense and is functioning duratively. This tense emphasizes that an action began in the past and continues in the future.

36. Jesus doesn't say "just be"; He says *"come unto me"* (Mt. 11:28). God's Word doesn't say, "I can"; it says "I can do all things *through him who strengthens me* (Phil. 4:18). Jesus says to love *him first* and to *love our neighbors as much as we love ourselves* (Mt. 22:37-39). Jesus tells us if we are not on the narrow path we *are* lost (Mt. 7:13-14). God's Word says our sinful flaws are ugly and we need to be washed from them (1 Cor. 6:9-11).

37. *Satana* is found in the genitive case, which is functioning to specify source.

38. *Jeopardy!* Directed by Clay Jacobsen. NBC, 1964–present.

39. *Echeis* is in the present tense, functioning progressively. When a verb in the present tense functions progressively, it stresses enduring action.

40. *Kai* functions an adversative conjunction. An adversative conjunction is placed between two opposites to present an emphatic, opposing idea.

41. *Kai* is functioning epexegetically (as an additional definition) to further clarify and explain the seven spirits of God. We could actually translate it as "namely." (The seven spirits of God *namely* the seven stars).

42. *Gregoreo* is found in the present tense and the imperative mood, meaning that Jesus is commanding them to urgent, continued watching.

43. *Stērizo* is used in the aorist tense and functions ingressively. An ingressive aorist focuses on the beginning of an action.

44. *Star Wars III, Revenge of the Sith*, directed by George Lucas (2005; 20th Century Fox).

45. *Dedōka* is being used in the perfect tense. The perfect tense describes an event that takes place in the past with its results continuing into the future.

46. *Etērēsas* and ērnēsō are found in the aorist tense.

47. *Kratei* is found in the imperative mood.

48. *Ho*, in both instances, serves as an article of par excellence. An article of par excellence sets something into a class all by itself. It presents an extreme version of something.

49. "Amen" (*amen*) in the Greek is a word that is used to express a strong affirmation. Here, it simply means "true and unchangeable support." Jesus was called "*the* Amen" because of his trustworthiness to keep his promises.

50. "Me" (*emou*) is found in the genitive case and it is being used with the preposition "from" (*para*). This makes the statement strong and emphatic.

51. *Zēleue* is found in the present tense and in the imperative mood. Present imperatives can mean urgent, continued action.

52. The word "stand" (*hestēka*) is found in the perfect tense. The perfect tense implies a past action that has a present result.